the Intuitive Adventure

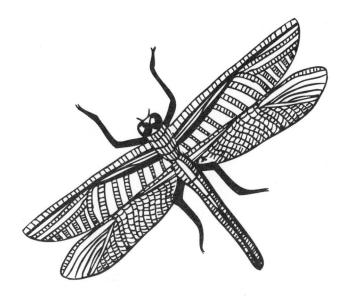

THE MAGIC OF FOLLOWING WHERE YOUR SOUL LEADS

SHANNON COX   Illustrated by NATALIE O'BRIEN

REDFeather™
MIND | BODY | SPIRIT

4880 Lower Valley Road, Atglen, PA 19310

Library of Congress Control Number: 2020943795

Type set in Gotham/Garton

ISBN: 978-0-7643-6193-7
Printed in China

Published by REDFeather Mind, Body, Spirit
An imprint of Schiffer Publishing, Ltd.
4880 Lower Valley Road | Atglen, PA 19310
Phone: (610) 593-1777; Fax: (610) 593-2002
E-mail: Info@redfeathermbs.com | Web: www.redfeathermbs.com

For our complete selection of fine books on this and related subjects, please visit our website at www.redfeathermbs.com. You may also write for a free catalog.

REDFeather Mind Body Spirit's titles are available at special discounts for bulk purchases for sales promotions or premiums. Special editions, including personalized covers, corporate imprints, and excerpts, can be created in large quantities for special needs. For more information, contact the publisher.

We are always looking for people to write books on new and related subjects. If you have an idea for a book, please contact us at proposals@schifferbooks.com.

You are infinitely loved.

Contents

Introduction

ive years ago I believed that being happy meant looking to those around me and ensuring their needs were met. It meant being caring and kind and ensuring that you always pushed yourself to do your best. Inside, I believe the answers I sought were in those around me who seemed to know what they were doing. While listening to these answers, pushing myself, and trying to be all I "needed" to be, I found I had inadvertently pushed myself beyond what my body was capable of. I never thought that was even possible, until I was in the hospital, with my legs no longer functioning normally and the doctors unsure how to help me heal.

I turned to a number of alternative methods until I stumbled across a collection of intuitive tools. I discovered more about my body: the stories I had inadvertently stored as to how capable I was and how I viewed myself and indeed the world around me. I learned that there was a wealth of information available under the surface and that I have access to my own answers. Indeed we all do. This journey helped me trust myself and step out into the world, not aware of where I was necessarily headed, but knowing that somehow I was supported throughout this. I wouldn't call it an easy path in any shape or form, but it has certainly been rewarding. While accessing my soul's guidance, I have found a way that I can choose to see the good in myself and trust the path I am following. This journey has allowed me to see I no longer have to fear how I see myself, or saying what I truly want for fear of going against those I love and care about—that somehow, the journey I have taken has led me to precisely where I am meant to be, following what lights me up as I listen to my own internal guidance.

I was unaware that I could choose to believe in myself so eloquently. At nineteen, I was wanting to find a way to prove to the world, and myself, that I was enough. I had just moved after finishing school and was working several casual jobs in the tourist town of Port Douglas in Far North Queensland in Australia. During the day I could be found working at a tour desk or souvenir shop, while at night I was waitressing at a local restaurant and then proceeding to the nightclubs afterward, hoping I would meet someone who could light up my world. I had been moving between flats, falling out with a number of friends, and had been in this cycle for over a year, feeling incredibly disconnected. I had met one guy who I thought was adorable, yet it turned out he was only interested in a casual relationship and my closest friend was dealing with her abusive boyfriend—along with the fact that I was drinking heavily, having many casual relationships and in turn not caring or respecting myself in any way. It was a time where I felt like I had fallen out of love with who I was in every way possible.

It was only when the local newspaper reported how I had been caught drunk driving, with my full name and age, that I was ready to disappear. The same week, my girlfriend and I talked about leaving town, and I realized I was quite happy to escape. We packed a small bag with a couple of items in it each and proceeded to hitch-hike that very evening to the closest capital city, Brisbane, which is over 1,200 miles (some 2,000 km) away. We arrived early Sunday morning with no plan of what to do next, except contact a kind family member who had offered us accommodation for a couple of weeks. We somehow landed a position in door-to-door sales, selling telephone accounts. Slowly, we scraped enough money together to rent a little house, trying to find a way to get enough for food and catch the train to work.

I called my parents to ask for help, and they offered to fly me home, and I point-blank refused. I couldn't admit that I had made a mistake or return to the same set of problems as before. I ended up hocking my stereo and finding a nice share house in the suburbs, landing a well-paying job with a software company. I connected with a few old school friends in Brisbane and felt like I had found my feet. Most weekends we would be found out on the town, and it was at one of the Brisbane pubs that I met a guy who showed me his sensitive side, making me laugh and feel comfortable, while reminding me how beautiful I was.

Shaun and I fell for each other quite quickly and ended up moving in together into his funky little house in Fruitgrove with his brother and Staffordshire terrier named Zeus. We enjoyed being in each other's company . . . cruising around in his old Holden Premier listening to old tunes, delivering me to work each day with bruffin in hand (a delicious breakfast muffin with bacon and eggs), or just hanging out on the deck, playing cards and talking about random goings on. His group of friends welcomed me in, and I found a group that made me feel like I belonged. We were married within a couple of years, buying our own home on acreage on the outskirts of Brisbane, and moved in with now two dogs and one feisty cat. I had truly left my party ways behind and was enjoying working at a local travel agency booking holidays, while discovering a long list of places I wanted to travel to. I also was ready to start our own family and started dreaming of ways we could make it all possible.

It was 2008. We had been trying for a number of years to conceive a child, and although Shaun was happy operating his own excavator business, I was now managing the local travel agency store and was hoping to find a way for my life to be less stressful. We took a trip away to a collection of nearby cabins dotted along the mountainside with my in-laws, along with my brother-in-law and his wife. It was here our lives began to catapult into a completely new direction. It was as the wine flowed and we all shared our hopes for a quieter life that we looked at the cottages around us and visualized the way our life could be with children and working together, while creating a beautiful space for holiday makers and their families.

Within a few weeks my father-in-law had decided he wished to purchase a similar business to this and was wondering who was interested in coming in with him and his wife. The conversations were getting serious, and it was as we were traveling to a number of possible businesses that Shaun and I discovered we were expecting our first child. Within a number of whirlwind months, we had sold our home and found ourselves moved to a nearby rugged wine country with a handful of cottages, one parsley farm, and a little man about to arrive.

I fell in love with our garden when we arrived, with its cherry trees, crabapples, and hydrangeas surrounding our small but simple worker's cottage. We painted our nursery and put together the cot, myself dreaming of ways I could work in the sunlit office while our son played at my feet. As a family, we had discussed jewelry-making courses and photography workshops while we planted, cleaned, and occasionally picked our little parsley farm once a fortnight.

It was as our son Aiden arrived that the realization of what was involved with our business unfolded. Parsley picking was a daily job, with all members of the family apart from myself down in the fields from 5 a.m. Once this was finished, there was time for lunch before heading to the cottages to clean them for the upcoming arrivals. I struggled with how to help while nursing our young man. I was confident and comfortable with the marketing, web design, and handling the phones, yet, as I walked into the cottages or into the fields, my confidence eroded, and I did not know how to help those around me the way I felt was needed.

I would see those working from early hours, including my now heavily pregnant sister-in-law expecting her first, and I realized that I was not the type of person they needed in this business. I was thoroughly enjoying setting up the internet presence of our holiday cottages and found a way to increase our bookings fairly dramatically. I also began finding ways to offer new services through the cottages, such as massages or romance packages. And yet, no matter which way I looked at it, I felt I was not helping as much as I should be. My work seemed light and enjoyable without the pressure of early mornings, long hours, and repetitive jobs. By the time Aiden was a few months old, it seemed fair that I was cottage cleaning while the others were in the fields. I remember walking down to the cottage with a baby monitor in hand and arriving to the same cottage I had cleaned only a handful of days ago, distraught that there was no real way I could stop this cycle without leaving. I enjoyed planning for the future, creating a space where I could grow with those around me and find what lights us up. In this space, I believed there was no future that made me feel excited or even content. I found myself caught in this story that I was not enough, and no matter which way I looked at it, what I had to offer was unneeded in this space. The hardworking ethos that surrounded me felt constricting rather than inspiring, and I found myself dreaming of how I could escape with my husband and son in the middle of the night.

I felt overwhelmed at the prospect of letting down the people around me. My quaint brochure of our purchased lifestyle was in pieces as I came to the realization that what we had anticipated was not the "dream" we had purchased. As we sat down with the rest of the family to discuss the full situation, we were thankful my husband's family chose to stay regardless if we chose to or not. Shaun and I both came to the conclusion that we needed another option that gave us more freedom.

It was over a year until we found something that suited our needs and desires, when a local motel and steakhouse came on to the market. Shaun and I suggested to the family of taking on the management side, and we were looking forward to being in a position where we could grow this business. As our families agreed and signed the contract, we were surprised to discover we were expecting our second child. We were shocked to find this happened with only two days of trying, compared to five years with our first-born; however, with the wheels in motion, we began planning for how our extended family would fit into our upcoming venture.

We moved into the house attached to our business and found we enjoyed showcasing just how much the local area had to offer, whether it was the local orchards, the fresh-cheese farm houses, the picturesque country lanes, or the walks in the local national parks. We found ourselves also reveling in the freedom of operating this business in the way we felt worked best for us and what we had to offer.

My husband and I began to settle in with the operational side of the business, particularly as many groups arrived to visit what the region had to offer. In the morning, Shaun would be found in the kitchen cooking their breakfast, while I would be serving and clearing plates, generally with at least one child resting on my hip. Our beautiful daughter, Georgie, had arrived, and life became busy with toddlers, buses, newborns, and coordinating staff and cleaners.

This motel was over fifty years old, and although the rooms were simple and clean, they were refurbished in the late eighties with pink tiles and light-gray walls. I remember asking out loud if somehow we could have a new motel; it would assist my marketing duties to be so much simpler. We could have modern and stylish rooms, attract new groups and tourists, and be proud of our business even more.

At this point, intuition for me was something I had heard of randomly but never utilized. And yet, for some unknown reason, I started noticing the number 11 everywhere, sometimes two or three times a day. Whether it was 11:11 on the clock next to the bed or 4:11, perhaps 3:11, on the clock in the car. This continued for weeks and then months. I remember mentioning this to my husband, wondering what this could possibly mean.

Late in 2013, I had just grabbed my two little ones out of the shower and found them wrapped around my legs as the lights of the building flickered in and out. As Shaun wandered around outside to see why this had happened, he felt a little electric current in his thongs. The power line was down in the driveway, and as he headed to the carport to get cover from the rain, he realized the entire roof was also missing. A tornado had come into Stanthorpe, taking down a number of large pine trees and a stable roof before crossing the highway and taking our entire motel roof off, scattering it between nearby streets and the local golf course.

Air-conditioner units were distributed across the backyard, and roof insulation could be seen wrapped around the trees, and yet our house and restaurant was untouched. Even the kids' toys in the backyard had barely moved. The local SES (State Emergency Services) were working late into the night tying down tarps over roof beams, hoping to stop the rain from entering into the motel rooms.

As the sun rose, Shaun and I wandered from room to room, trying to understand what had happened. We had holes in walls and ceilings, as well as saturated beds, and virtually every room was sodden. And yet, everyone was safe; it just turned out that our motel rooms needed to be pretty much entirely rebuilt.

It was only when we saw the local newspapers with our story and the images of what had happened that we realized the significant date this had all occurred. The eleventh day of the eleventh month. I was sure we were being forewarned, with the number eleven being seen everywhere, and was trying to wrap my head around the idea that somehow someone was aware this was coming beforehand and how that could be possible.

The insurance company could cover all of the repairs, as well as the loss of income, even our housekeeper's wages, as we waited for the motel to reopen. It seemed odd to find how many silver linings arrived with this event. All our motel rooms were refurbished, even with new bathrooms, curtains, and carpet. Brand-new air conditioners and microwaves, down to the lamps and toasters. Our reception was closed for a number of months, and Shaun and I enjoyed a leisurely life with no motel guests and just operating the restaurant while organizing all the replacement fittings.

However, strange events continued to occur in my world. It was one night, clearing the table, that threw me. I heard ever so gently the words in my mind . . . "I will not see my son get married." I stopped instantly what I was doing and concentrated on these words, trying to understand where they'd even come from. I couldn't understand why I would think this . . . and began to suspect maybe it was true. Perhaps this was another weird, crazy message coming through like the number elevens I had seen everywhere? My husband held me tight that night, while I wondered if I now had a time limit on my life.

Waking groggily and sleep-deprived, we learned the next morning that a colleague had passed away the night before, leaving behind his young nine-year-old son. I didn't understand how this could happen, and my husband was completely shell-shocked. I could see he was trying to grapple with how this was possible or what it even meant.

But life continued on; our motel was almost ready to reopen. The furniture had arrived with all the accessories, and we were busy lifting and moving the chairs and beds into the motel rooms. My husband lifted me off the truck and twirled me around before placing me down on the ground. He had taken me completely by surprise, and I found my whole body panicked and my legs went to jelly. I remember staring up at him, holding his arm, trying to simply hold up my weight, unable to balance, let alone walk.

Our doctor booked an MRI and blood tests while I tried to continue with our life as normal as possible. When I took my son to school, and my bladder gave way, it was enough to terrify and mortify me at the same time. It's funny; at the time I could deal with dodgy legs, but the idea of no bladder control left me feeling completely unsexy. I was really scared. I didn't know what this was at all. The only thing I knew was something was very wrong with me. The words multiple sclerosis were thrown around, and yet, surprisingly, my MRI tests kept coming back normal.
By the time the final MRI test came back healthy, I was walking only with the assistance of another person. I was wearing an incontinence pad, and deep inside I had this horrible feeling that no one would know how to help me. The local hospital organized an ambulance to the Toowoomba Neurological Department, where they advised they had seen this once a year or so and that it was a stress disorder.

His words were something along the line of "running a business can be stressful." I was furious and felt so alone. I had never ever heard of someone losing the ability to walk or control their bladder due to stress. At this time he recommended I go home. All I could keep thinking was if my home and business was making me sick, then how could I get better if they sent me home. I was desperately seeking answers on how to fix this, on how to get better. And yet, I was feeling as though the nurses and doctors were looking at me, knowing this was all pretty much in my head.

While I was still in hospital, I tried pushing my body each day and began testing numerous theories myself. I tried walking to the nearby corner shop. If this was "all in my head" as I thought, then I should be able to control it. I got there, albeit quite slowly. I grabbed some sushi and went to buy a notepad and pen. As I asked the assistant where I could find a pen, I realized my legs had had enough for the moment. I was not going to make it to where they were kept. As she grabbed the pen for me, my awkward gait started again, and I shuffled my body back to the table and chairs outside while berating myself for thinking I could do this. After weighing all my options, I forlornly concluded I would have to catch a taxi less than 1/4 mile (a mere 400 meters) back to the hospital.

As I came back into the ward, I found I was being moved again. Originally placed in my own private room, I was then moved to a group ward, and now I was to be moved to the day surgery ward to stay overnight. With each move my legs gave way, as did my trust that the hospital was able to help me recover. The nurse helped pack my belongings, wheeling me in to the next ward while I panicked that I could not find a way to stop this pattern. For many reasons, I associated the moving of wards with not being believed that I was unwell or belonged in the hospital.

The next day I felt better and decided to take my wheelchair out for a walk. I could push it until I felt tired, and then I could sit as I recovered. I checked out the hospital library and was super excited to find a dear friend was working there. We sat chatting away for hours about life, about the people we knew, and he gave me a wonderful collection of movies to fill in the hours. As he left, I realized I had not thought once about not making it to the toilet. It was with this that the thought entered my mind that maybe I could heal this. That afternoon I was moved again from the day surgery ward to the transit ward. Again, I saw my gait dramatically change as I was moved.

The next morning, I had two dear girlfriends visit me. I was so excited to see them, and so exhausted at the same time. I could see the look of pained surprise as they saw me step out of the wheelchair and do my beautiful gaited walk to give them a hug. The neurologist was there at the same time and noted he did not have to worry about depression with me. He could see the excitement written all over my face. We grabbed the wheelchair and headed out of the ward. "Do you want to head to the cafeteria?" asked Sarah. I looked at her incredulously. We were in Toowoomba. And to any regional country girl, that meant shopping. My two girlfriends looked at me in the wheelchair and then grinned.

I remember the exhilaration as we flew down into the parking lot and pulled open the Land Cruiser boot, trying to figure out how to remove the drip stand from the wheelchair. It was a glorious sunny day, and we headed to the biggest shopping center in town. I was so excited to get some thongs and eat real food. I so badly wanted to be able to walk, but within a couple of hours, I could barely keep my head up. I was just so physically exhausted.

Our last stop was a clothing store; I was randomly looking at a few goodies when my phone rang. I answered it to find the nurse from my ward wondering where I was. I explained we were just out in the garden, hoping she could not hear the pop music in the background. We giggled as we headed back, trying to figure out how we could get away with this. The end conclusion was to push the ward doors open and fling my wheelchair in while making a quick escape.

In the end it was a bit more civilized. Two big hugs, and I climbed into bed exhausted, passing out within minutes.

On my last day, my neurologist did a couple of final tests. Normally when they touched my feet by surprise, I would start shaking, kind of like an epileptic fit. He showed me how when I was prepared, I could stop this from happening. I was sent home with antianxiety medication and a date with a psychologist.

My husband was beautiful and protective as I came home. He took on the management side of the motel, while the kids covered me in kisses. I had this moment with my body where I promised I would work out how we could get along again, and I went with happiness as the new goal.

It was a journey trying to understand what had happened.
I had lived my life thinking I knew exactly what I wanted, and here I was feeling as though none of the plans I wanted were possible. I thought if I worked hard at what I loved, I would be rewarded and have a healthy, successful life. And here I was unable to function or achieve in any of the ways I was used to. I thought my life was here to teach me how to be a good person, but here I was being shown that if I did what I thought was "good," I would become sick. Everything I thought I knew was thrown out the window, and I began again.

I thought maybe mindfulness would help, meditation, perhaps yoga! Yet, it was when I stumbled across a book in my local library that I felt as though I could be in charge of my life again. It was called *Energy Medicine* by Donna Eden, and it spoke of healing your body through understanding the energy of it, such as chakras, auras, and meridians. It also used muscle testing as one form of asking your body what it needed. I felt as though I had discovered the magical cure I was searching for. I immersed myself in learning about ways to structure all the information that was being thrown at me. Why did I become overwhelmed in certain situations? Why did I desire time with some and refuse to be around other people? What would happen if I chose another option than my normal patterns?

My beautiful body helped me through this process. Each time I became overwhelmed, I found myself tensing up. This then started me thinking of what had just happened before to trigger this reaction. I became aware of my stressors and looked for clues within my energy structures to change my internal programming. Each event helped me learn about what I was ready to let go of, and the reactions I no longer wanted in my world. I began healing myself.

It might be something as simple as cleansing my chakras each day as I showered, or using an essential oil to calm myself. I wanted to learn more and delved into shamanism and retrieving soul pieces. Each scenario, I felt as though I had nothing to lose and everything to gain from giving it a go. I learned how to release emotions attached to old memories, to change the way I saw myself and the decisions I had made in the past. But most importantly, I learned to forgive myself and the people around me.

It was when a girlfriend and I decided to write a diary that it became clear to me how many of these tools had played a role in my world. Each week in the diary, I wrote a simple tip, and each month we delved further into tools to help people connect with themselves. As we finished the diary, it became clear to me just how many tools I had collected along the way, and the feedback from our diary showed just how useful they were.

I wanted people to understand these tools, and for anyone who wanted to learn more, to have somewhere to go to get all this information. And this is how this book arrived into the world. I had been collecting all of these tools to heal myself, but also how to play with my intuition without judgment or fear. The thought that kept coming up was this: If I am intuitive, how do I make this useful in my world? What can I use it for? And so I played—whether it was with food, cleansing, being creative, or changing the way I saw myself and the world.

I truly believe we can change the way we see ourselves and what we are capable of. We can go out there and create a life where we feel worthy, loved, creative, and caring. Where we can see the good in ourselves and the people around us.

I realized my life is indeed whatever I want it to be. I can ask for a better relationship with my husband and children and see it arrive. I can connect with a business idea that I believe in, and uncover ways to take it where I want it to go, while ditching the beliefs within that are limiting me. The beauty in this soul-led journey is realizing whatever lands in your world is there to help you in one way or another. This helped me relax and trust myself, trying whatever grabs my interest without fear of failing.

Oh, my gosh, it is one hell of an adventure. The beauty in finding your voice over all the external noise is key to unlocking the life that you have dreamed of. The intuitive world is all about uncovering what is exciting for you as a soul to discover, and how to embrace a world that truly supports and rewards you for being you.

Welcome

his little book is here so that you can learn how to have fun with your intuition. To help you play, delve, and dabble away while finding your own answers. Start with the tools section, then see what takes your interest from there. There is no need to read this book in any particular order. In fact, the simplest way is to flick to a random page and see what it says.

As you play and delve, your intuitive skills will naturally grow. This ability is available in all of us by trusting and relaxing, allowing the process to unfold as you learn more about what you are capable of. Whenever you find something is difficult or hard to navigate, take a breather. It just means not all of the pieces are in place to make this happen, yet.

You have indeed chosen this life and have a number of guides and souls that you have asked to assist you along the way. You chose your parents, who you thought would give you the best chance to complete your soul desires for this life. You chose particular souls to help guide you at pivotal moments in your life. You also have spirit guides, which are souls who are here to help you from "the other side."

Open your mind and heart to these new adventures and enjoy. Just by opening yourself up to these opportunities, you are creating change. Your soul-led adventure is just beyond this page.

Am I Intuitive?

believe we are all born intuitive. You have been using this natural skill, possibly unconsciously, for your entire life.

This book is designed just to help you see these intuitive moments more clearly. There are a couple of important things to note before you start.

Your body is naturally intuitive. You can access this information with the activities in this book and tap into whatever your body is feeling. You could be experiencing some tension about a conversation, stressing about a situation, or simply feeling overwhelmed. Your mind may be saying, "Logically this does not makes sense" while your body is intuitively saying "yes."
Everything is going to be okay. Wherever you are, whatever you are facing, everything happens for a reason. You do not have to be afraid. You do not have to have all the answers yet. Trust in the process of life.

That's it. You have all the required skills and answers to now relax, play, and delve.

Let's have some fun . . .

Let Us Begin

hen you connect with your intuition, you are actually connecting to subtle energies. These can be your own emotions and memories, the space you are working in, where you have come from, and the people around you. It is easier, especially when you are beginning to play with these energies, to start with a cleansed space and body. Ready for some fun?

1. Choose a space to practice where you can relax undisturbed.
2. A simple way to cleanse your space is to set an intention as you light a candle, such as "Please cleanse this space energetically" or "I invite peace, love, and joy into this space." Whatever you feel comfortable with. See page 72 for more ideas on cleansing your space.
3. To cleanse your body, you can simply have a shower or bath and cleanse your aura (see page 71).
4. Sit on the ground with your eyes closed and your palms facing upward. See what you can feel in your space. Try stating the following: "Please raise my vibration to a 10." What changes do you feel in your body?
5. Take a few deep breaths to connect into the subtle energies around you.

Now open your eyes. You are ready to have a play! Feel free to flick through this book, if you haven't already, to find a page that takes your fancy, and then delve, dabble, and enjoy.

Tap Into Your Body

ave you ever felt unsure what you are supposed to do next? Whether all the responsibility has fallen on your shoulders to make a decision, or you just feel lost within all the options.

Every time you are faced with a decision, choose what makes you feel good. This means that as a thought enters your mind, see what your body is intuitively feeling.

A simple exercise to tap into feeling what your body is trying to say to you . . .

Think of a food you love. Imagine popping it into your mouth. As you are savoring each mouthful, how does your body feel? Take note of any physical sensations you can feel.
Like a warmth in your belly or heart, maybe tingles on your back?

Now imagine popping something into your mouth that you really don't like. Where are you feeling these negative sensations? What do they feel like? Maybe a tightness, a sickly feeling?

When you have a decision to make, imagine each option and see which feels the most enjoyable.

Follow whatever makes you feel lighter and happier.

Automatic Writing

 began writing a few years back when I felt overwhelmed and upset. I had all of these emotions inside me that I didn't completely understand, and writing seemed to help me calm myself and see what was affecting me.

I then read one day about automatic writing, where you can access your intuition by using your pen and paper. As I practiced, I found the words naturally came out in second person . . . "You will find what you are looking for."

I may have hidden my journals at this stage, as I felt they would have seemed ludicrous. And yet, whenever I read these back, I just felt this calming sense of love.

Now it's your turn! Start by grabbing a pen and notebook. Find a quiet space for you to relax and connect (see page 28). Light a candle and take a few deep breaths.

Think of a question (if you have one) and then write on the sheet "My intuition would like to say——." See what comes out of your pen.

Give yourself full permission to write complete nonsense. It does not matter if it sounds like a foreign language. Just do not filter or dismiss anything that comes forward.
If nothing seems to be coming out of your pen, try writing the

sentence: "My intuition would like to say——" over and over until something more comes out of your pen.

You have the ability to connect with your intuition; just be patient and give yourself time to learn how.

Try a question that you have been asking yourself for a while, or flip through the pages of this book for inspiration on question ideas.

Intentions

 When you set an intention for the day, you are inviting the universe to allow your desires to arrive into your world. It is truly magical watching this happen. The joy is not knowing how this intention will arrive, and yet they do.

I start when I wake up by thinking, "What I would love to see today?" A heart-to-heart conversation with my husband? A full cleanse of my space? Maybe a fun and lighthearted catch-up with a friend to release the pressure I have at the moment or to feel more at ease with my schedule. You may ask to connect with what has been playing on your mind that you would like help with.

You do not have to worry about how you will make this happen. No step-by-step plans or schedules are necessary. Just invite this opportunity into your world and see what happens. This is setting your vibration to automatically invite these intentions into your world. By releasing control on the "hows," you are allowing the universe to take care of this.

Change it up each day, play, try different intentions, and then watch what happens.

Believe what you seek is very naturally on its way to you.

READY TO LEARN MORE?

Time your intention setting with something you already do each morning, (e.g., before you get out of bed, when you have a cuppa or brush your teeth). Make this your new daily habit.

Write a monthly intention for your journey. Read your previous intentions afterward to see just how far you have transitioned.

Hopping in the car? Think about what you would like to experience while out and about: fun for the whole family, a car park close to where you are headed, less traffic, clothing sale with sexy clothes you love. Try being specific and then not so specific. What happens?

Relax and Believe

saw a quote the other day, on a Target shirt of all places! "The Universe Is Your Playground."

What if they are right?

What if this life is about playing? About learning and discovering? Making mistakes and picking yourself up. Trusting that there is something bigger than yourself at play, and everything is happening for a reason.

What if?

You could relax a little. Trust that everything is going along to plan, even if you don't 100% know what that plan is.

What if the universe had your back?

And it knew what you deeply desired. You could put your dreams out there for the world to see, and watch them unfold in your life.

What if I told you this is all true?

You can relax, my friend, because the universe does indeed have your back. Everything around you is happening for a reason. And you are going to be okay. You are going to be more than okay. Trust and relax and take this ride. Because I promise you, it is one hell of a ride. You will discover that magic is real, that wishes can come true, and that you are beautiful just as you are.

make a
wish.

Body Swaying

 love muscle testing. It is a simple way to get clear answers from your body without your mind getting involved. I find my mind is not always aware of everything that is at play, and by muscle testing I can tap into my intuition. This activity involves swaying your whole body to answer yes or no questions.

Imagine there is a string connected from the top of your head that holds your body up like a puppet. Stand with your feet shoulder width apart, bend your knees slightly, and release any tension in your body.

Start with a simple statement, such as "My name is (insert your name here)."

Relax your body and see how it moves. Your body will naturally move forward if it agrees with the statement and move backward if it disagrees.

Sometimes you will get a sensation of moving sideways—like it's neither a no nor a yes. In this case, try rewording the question to see if you can get a clearer answer.

You can use this for almost any question your soul is ready to answer. I found this to be a simple way to know which of my chakras needed a cleanse, as well as what beliefs I am ready to release.

Life Choices

 t some point before being born, you were presented with a number of choices. An opportunity to choose what experiences will give you the tools you need to achieve your soul's purpose?

I read a beautiful book called *Journey of Souls: Case Studies of Life between Lives* by Michael Newton, a hypnotherapist who interviewed people about the period between death and rebirth. These interviews have been printed as case studies and show a pattern between each description.

What was fascinating was how each person chose their reason to be reborn on Earth, and how they chose the best place, family, and experiences to make this all happen. What if everything that is happening around you is happening for a reason? What if there is a benefit for every misfortune? What if these experiences gave you the tools you need to achieve your soul's desire in your life?

This would mean your "imperfections" have a purpose. Your guilt and shame are no longer needed. Your beauty is in knowing you are not supposed to be perfect. You are supposed to be you, with all the twist and turns that have taken you to where you are today.

And this version of you is the one that can achieve your soul's desires.

Visualizations

isualization is the single easiest way to transform your life. Big call, I know. By visualizing something already here, you are able to change your vibration. I know we haven't touched much on vibrations; however, the basic "law of attraction" theory is you can attract whatever matches your own vibration. Your beliefs, ideas, and thoughts create a vibration, and this will attract what you believe is true and possible. This is great if you are optimistic and believe in the good around you. However, if you are having difficulties believing something is possible, visualizing is a great way to change this.

The beauty of visualizations is you can do this anytime and anywhere, though preferably find a spot you can be undisturbed.

Visualizations also give you the ability to feel and experience what you desire. As you delve into your visualization you may find your dreams become clearer and more succinct. You also have the ability to home in on what you want the most, and to discard any parts of your dream that you discover are not actually aligned with you.

For example, you may wish your business or career to be highly successful, and yet you may also want a more balanced approach with your life. Try visualizing what this lifestyle would actually look like. Take this one step further and visualize what success actually means to you. What is your ideal income? How would you like to give back to the world? How would you like to spend time with your friends and family? How do you see your weekends and evenings? Imagine this in all its glory. You may find you need to fine-tune your ideas. Ensure whatever you are visualizing makes you feel happy and excited. This means you are aligned with your desire and not choosing someone else's ideal.

Your soul work: When thinking of your career or business, visualize how you would like your ideal day "working" to pan out.

Looking for a new home: It is time for a virtual, visual tour. Imagine opening the front door and walking through your personalized dream home. Go through the kitchen, the living room, and the

bedrooms, and stand in the backyard drinking in the view. Imagine interacting with those you love and how you would like to spend your time in this space.

Your last day: Fast forward to many, many years from now, to your last day in this life. When you think back to what happened in your life, what are the moments you treasure? What do you see that makes you feel proud? Visualize all the moments that made you who you are on this day and why they are important to you.

Your Spirit Guide

ou are not alone on this journey through life, gorgeous one. You have invited a few souls to join you on this voyage tohelp you achieve your purpose in this lifetime. These souls are known as your spirit guides.

Your guides are a little bit different from your soul or higher self. They are like a guardian angel who has chosen to work with you on this adventure. The best description I have found is this: if you are in a forest and looking for answers, your soul is on one of the mountains offering assistance, while your guides are on the peaks with another viewpoint.

They know you incredibly well and want you to grow and expand in this lifetime. If you are reading this page, then you are ready to connect with your spirit guide. Feel whatever activity below resonates to you, and enjoy.

READY TO LEARN MORE?

Take the time now to connect with your guide. It can be as simple as meditating in a quiet space and saying hi.

You can ask your guides any question and receive their response through automatic writing (see page 32).

Try your pendulum to ask simple yes-and-no questions about your guides.

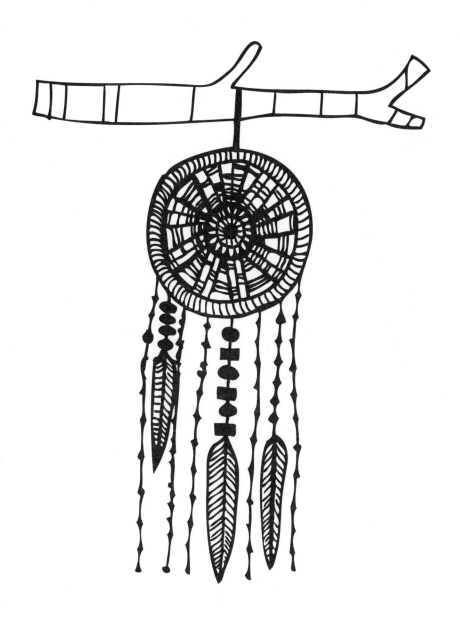

Pendulum

 beautiful, physical way to connect with your intuition is with a pendulum.

Find a necklace with a pendant or stone on it. I used one gifted to me by a close girlfriend.

Hold the necklace gently between your thumb and finger, with the pendant hanging down.

State the following: "I ask my soul and spirit guides to assist me."

Ask to be shown a yes . . . the pendulum will swing in a particular shape, such as a clockwise circle or backward and forward. Then ask to see what a no looks like, and then, last of all, a maybe. Now it is time to just play,

Start by asking simple questions to see what your intuition answers with. If this activity is not working at the moment, maybe not everything is in place yet to make this work. Try another activity and give this activity space until it feels right.

READY TO LEARN MORE?

Use the alphabet to work out your guides' names. You can speed this up by sorting your letters (e.g., write out your alphabet—A through to G on row one, H–M on row two, then N–S and T–Z, etc.). Ask which row first and then the letter.

Muscle Testing

 nce you are comfortable with body swaying, you may wish to find a way you can muscle-test unobtrusively, like when you are shopping or looking for lunch. It is time to try flick testing. This is a method of muscle testing that is quicker, and, bonus, you can do it anywhere.

With your nondominant hand, join your third finger and thumb as though you are about to flick your finger out.

You can begin with a simple statement, such as your name or age.

If the thumb and finger stay joined together, this shows your body's energy as strong, which means this statement is correct, while if the finger flicks, this shows your energy is not strong and your body disagrees.

Practice as much as you can, and play with how you ask the questions.

READY TO LEARN MORE?

Once you have this down pat, you can ask virtually anything. Try also varying the question in regard to perspective, such as from your soul or your body (e.g., "My soul believes this is a great idea for lunch?" "My body would like this for lunch?"). Muscle testing is a fun and easy way to get an intuitive answer quickly.

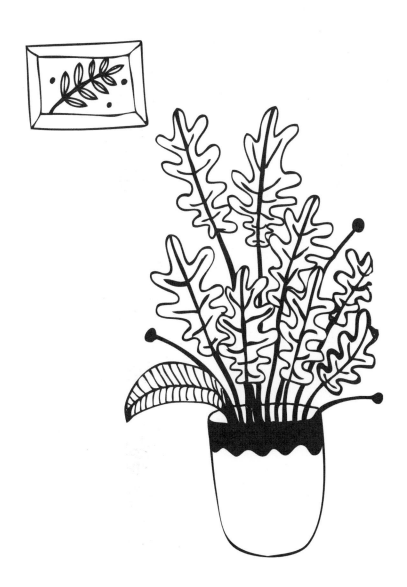

Universe "To-Do" List

There are times in our lives when we feel overwhelmed. There is so much to be done, so much responsibility that we place on our shoulders, and nowhere near enough time to get it all done.

This is a simple and beautiful activity, where you consciously release control over to the universe.

Take a piece of paper and jot down all the things you are happy for the universe to look after.

This can be anything, maybe something that is outside your control, asking for fresh ideas on how to tackle issues in your life or anything that has been on your to-do list for a while and hasn't happened for one reason or another.

I found when I handed these back to the universe, these "jobs" were often voluntarily done for me by someone else, solutions flew into my head randomly, or the issues somehow were resolved on their own.

The beauty came not from completing these tasks but by actually watching how they ended up happening so easily.

I find there is normally a reason why our "to-do" items have not been done yet.

Hand them over to the universe and unburden yourself.

Affirmations

or those of you who are not familiar with affirmations, these are the words we speak to ourselves day in and day out. The theory of the law of attraction is that you attract what you internally believe.

Ever had the thought "Why does this situation keep happening to me"? You are actually inadvertently sending out a vibration where you believe this event will continue.

In the same breath, if you believe the pain you are holding is no longer needed and you also believe that things are going to change for the better, you are ready to invite this change in.
Here are a few of my favorites that I have picked up along the way.

I no longer need to hold on.

I have everything I need to enjoy my here and now.

I have all the love I need in my heart.

I can relax and be me.

I invite my body to connect and realign to its perfection at a cellular level.

My business is continually thriving and exciting.

I am blessed with a beautiful family and wonderful friends. I invite wonder, joy, and magic into my world.

I acknowledge my own self-worth; my confidence is soaring.

I am a unique being, a one-of-a-kind artwork that can provide much enjoyment just from my very existence.

Positive affirmations are a simple way to invite the change you desire. Say them out loud whenever you desire. Write them on your walls, on Post-it notes, on your mirror or your desk; wherever you will see them often.

READY TO LEARN MORE?

Daily intention: Start each day by stating out loud what you wish to invite into your world.

Automatic writing: Write your own collection of affirmations.

Word search: Ask for inspiration that connects to how you are feeling today. This could be a passage in a book, an oracle card, or even just a magnet on the fridge.

Journal: Pop together a book with all the affirmations you connect with.

Cleanse Your Chakras

 love chakra cleansing. It has helped me grow so much and also understand more about my energetic body. Your chakras are a part of your energetic body, and when they are out of balance, they can affect your emotions. I started cleansing in the shower, in front of the fire, in the car, even before I went to sleep. Here are some simple ways to try this for yourself:

I started by using the body-swaying technique to work out which chakras needed to be cleansed (see page 39). Start by thinking about your base chakra and state, "This chakra is clean, clear, and balanced."

If you get a yes, this means it is clean and balanced. Feel free to move up to the next chakra. If you get a no, move your left hand in a circular motion over this chakra in a clockwise motion from your perspective (about the size of an extra-large dinner plate).

You may find that a memory or feeling may come to mind as you are cleaning. This could be what is blocking your chakra. Continue until you feel as though you have released this emotion. This could be a sense of your body relaxing. You can also ask for a sign that your chakra is cleaned, whether it is a smile or simply an inner knowing.

Once you feel relaxed and cleansed, shake your hands to release the negative energy, then reverse your circling motion to counterclockwise. This will allow the chakra go back to its normal flow.

Continue this until you feel relaxed (normally two to three minutes). Trust your intuition and go with whatever feels good to you. Once this is chakra is cleansed, move up to the next chakra, asking if it is cleansed and balanced.

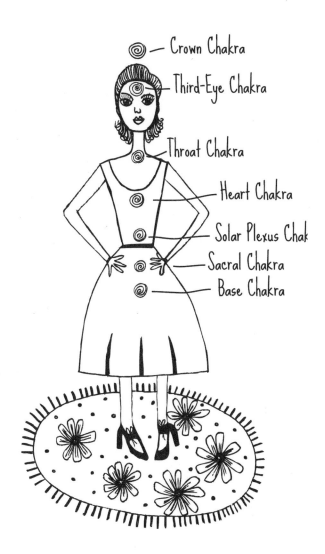

— Crown Chakra

— Third-Eye Chakra

— Throat Chakra

— Heart Chakra

— Solar Plexus Chak

— Sacral Chakra

— Base Chakra

Chakras

Base chakra (red): Located at the base of your spine. This chakra when balanced grounds you and provides stability. It is also related to your vitality and how you view yourself.

Sacral chakra (orange): Located below your navel. I think of this as the creative chakra, where enthusiasm, optimism, creativity, and problem-solving live.

Solar plexus chakra (yellow): Located above your navel. Your self-confidence is found here. When balanced, you find fun, self-belief, humor, intellect, and lightness.

Heart chakra (green): Located within your heart. This is your center for harmony, love, and acceptance and where you fall in love.

Throat chakra (blue): Located in your throat. You will find self-expression, creativity, transformation, communication, and judgment here.

Third-eye chakra (indigo): Located at the center of your forehead, where imagination, meditation, self-responsibility, inner strength, clairvoyance, calmness, creativity, artistic ability, and your intuition are housed.

Crown chakra (white/violet): Located on top of your head. You will find spirituality, self-knowledge, artistic abilities, acceptance, and bliss when this chakra is balanced.

Releasing Beliefs

nside your body are numerous beliefs. Some of these beliefs are beautiful and true, while there are other negative stories or thoughts that do not serve any purpose.

An example could be as simple as a time you may have fallen over. You overhear a comment that you are clumsy, and assume this is the truth.

Or you may have been told from a young age that dogs are dangerous or that rich people are mean. Some of these beliefs are harmless; however, deep down these may be affecting the decisions you make.

Next time you are upset, see if this is related to a belief. Write down all your pain and see if there is a belief you are holding on to that is simply not true. "I am not a good friend." "No one believes me." You may feel a tightening in your body when you think this thought.

Relax your body, then state out loud: "I release this feeling from my body." To add to the effect, visualize this leaving your body. "I imagine a wisp of air and feel this leave my body and float away out of my sight." It is as simple as that.

This can be done anywhere at anytime. This technique helped me believe in myself again. Whenever I get stuck, I focus on where I feel uncomfortable, and release this feeling from my body. Head to page 154 for more on this.

Meditation

his tool is a simple way to bring yourself back to the present moment. As you experience this consciousness, you will begin to experience a blissful state. Find a way you can bring this into your life as a daily habit to really experience the difference it can have on your life.

What you need: A quiet space where you will not be disturbed. Feel free to use candles if this relaxes you. Place your feet on the floor or sit cross-legged. (If you lie in bed, you may fall asleep!)

What next: Breathing is a very important part of meditating. Breathe deeply into your diaphragm through your nose, hold ,and then breathe out slowly through your mouth, shaped like an *o*. Pause for a beat before repeating.

While breathing in this manner, you have a number of options on how to meditate.

Sounds: Focus on the different sounds you can hear around you. The traffic, the creaks in the roof or the fridge. Become aware of the space around you while continuing your breathing.

Centering: Follow the instructions on page 65 for this.

Visualizations: Allow your mind to relax and create its own story for you to watch. This may be meeting your guides or soul, heading to a sacred space or the first place your mind thinks of.

The sky: Enjoy the emptiness of the sky in front of you. Any thoughts that bubble up into your consciousness, allow them to drift out of your view like a cloud.

Relaxing: Feel your body release all its tension. Start with your ankles relaxing, and progressively move up your body to the knees, thighs, hips, midsection, chest, arms, shoulders, neck, and head. Indulge in this relaxed state of your entire body.

Guided: If you are finding the above options difficult, then try a guided meditation. Use your intuition to guide yourself to the best option on that day.

Relaxation tip: If you find your mind jumping in with thoughts, focus on your breathing again and then try to think what the next thought will be. Enjoy the silence while your mind is occupied with this game.

Bring this as a habit for ten to twenty minutes per day to really feel the benefits.

This can be as simple as adding it to another morning habit such as before breakfast, when you wake up, or after you brush your teeth.

Rewrite the Story

hen we look back at our lives and what led us to this place, there may be regrets, blame, and thoughts that other people could have treated you better.

The part we may be overlooking is how all these things that happened helped define who you are today. These are your memories, and the easiest way to move on is to change the story by changing which parts you focus on.

Let's start by focusing on any positives from the situation, whether it is a willingness to fight harder for something important next time, a broader viewpoint, or even a greater understanding of what you love or what is important to you.

Take the time to go through any stories that stand out, and find some benefits from it happening exactly the way it did.

Another simple change is to rewrite the story completely by adding an element of fun or joy to a challenging memory. It can be as simple as adding some hot-pink balloons somewhere in your memory that distract you from what you no longer benefit from reliving. With one of my scariest memories as a child, I now think of my cat there with me. This simple distraction has changed the way I view these otherwise painful memories.

Try visualizing a new and improved story that focuses on the lessons and minimizes the pain.

Centering

This is a simple way to reconnect and align yourself.

Step into a quiet place, where you will be undisturbed. Even better if you can, step outside under a tree or on the grass.

Take some deep breaths, close your eyes, and relax your body.

I visualize a thick cord coming from my base chakra and heading deep down into the ground, wrapping itself around the center of the Earth as though it is locked in place.

Allow the energy of Mother Earth to come up through this cord into your body, all the way up your belly button and then back down into the ground, cleansing your energetic system.

Imagine your crown chakra opening up to the sky above. Visualize a white light streaming down through your crown, and once again allow this energy to come into your body in a U shape, down to your belly button and up again, cleansing your energy.

Continue this visualization through your breath. Bring in fresh expansive love with each breath in, and as you breathe out, release all that is no longer needed in your world.

When you are ready, open your eyes and allow yourself to take a moment to feel into your body in this present moment and see how you are feeling after this activity.

Soul Purpose

Before your life on Earth began, your soul existed. Just as when someone passes on, their soul continues.

Before you came to Earth, you designed this life. You invited a number of souls in to assist you, including your family members, your partner, and your friends.

Your chosen life is based on what your soul wishes to experience and how it wishes to grow. You are here to experience life with all the joy, adventure, pain, and anguish that comes with it. You are here to grow from this experience.

You also have come with a wealth of knowledge and a selection of interests that are your own. Finding your passion is combining your interests together to create your own unique viewpoint.

This means something different for every single person, and your unique journey is entirely yours. Embrace what is important to you and stay true to who you are.

Ready to learn more?

Read *The Secret language of Destiny* by Gary Goldschneider and Joost Elffers.

Ask for guidance from your intuition through automatic writing or a guided meditation.

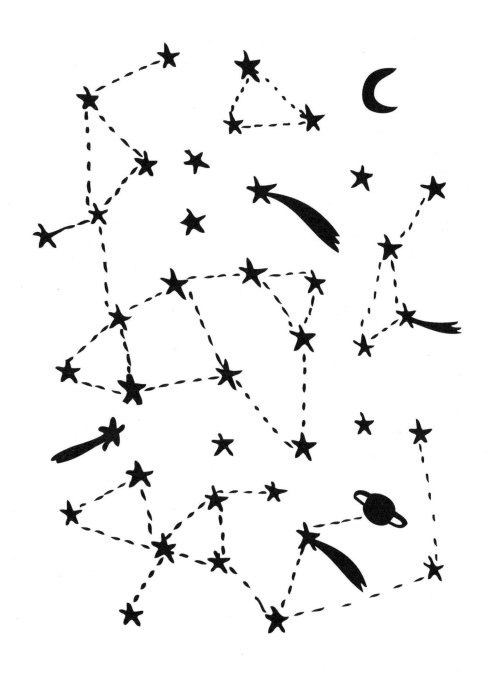

Cleansing

A bath or shower is a chance for you to ditch all the negative emotions that have arrived in your world each day. It is a beautiful way to unwind, relax, and clear your energy.

Play with these ideas during your next shower or bath, and tune into your body to feel how this affects your energy.

Crystals and shells: Personalize your space with whatever feels good.

Tea lights: A simple way to give the room a beautiful glow. Especially beautiful with a shower and the mist from the water.

Visualizations: Imagine the shower washing light all over you, cleansing your energy and washing away all negativity.

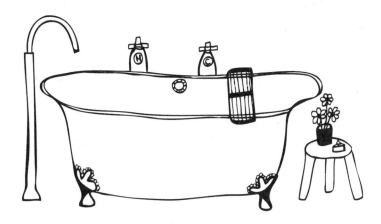

Chakra cleanse: Check intuitively if your chakras are clean, clear, and balanced, either while you are in the shower or before you hop in.

Exfoliate: Try using a bath scrub, loofah, or even just your towel when you dry as a mini exfoliant to cleanse your aura.

Massage oil / moisturizer: As you rub the oil or moisturizer on your skin, be thankful for all the amazing things your body is doing to keep you healthy.

Show your body love: Lather your hands up with soap and connect with your body while washing it by hand. At the same time, think about how many amazing things your body is doing for you at this moment. Give it a hug and be thankful for all you love about your body.

Essential oils: I use a couple of drops of lavender oil in my bath, which I find is really calming. Have a look at page 78 to learn more about choosing oils that resonate with your energetic self.

Epsom salts: Available in bulk at the local landscaping or livestock shop. A couple of cups to relax all the tension in your body. Heaven.

Music: Try your favorite instrumental or meditative music. Also binaural music to help you get into an alpha state. Before you go to sleep, your mind enters this state, similar to a light hypnotic state where you feel relaxed. This music is also a great way to tune into your intuition.

Bicarb soda: Perfect way to add little bubbles to your bath.

Feel Your Energy

These are my favorite ways to pick myself up, either when I am feeling flat or in need of a confidence boost before going on stage. They are also great before a job interview or a presentation.

Daily energy routine: Donna Eden has a fabulous daily routine that cleans and balances the energy in your body. Have a look on YouTube for her video clip (search Donna Eden's Daily Energy Routine).

Confidence booster: Standing like superman for just two minutes can change our level of confidence and chances of success as well as the chemicals in our blood. Amy Cuddy has a brilliant TED Talk (search "Your body language may shape who you are" by Amy Cuddy on Ted.com) that explains the science and studies behind these findings. You can try any power stance, including feet on the desk or arms on hips, for just two minutes. The beauty is it doesn't matter how unconfident you feel while doing these moves; there is still a huge impact.

Aura cleanse: Gently wave your arms around the space within 2 to 3 feet of your body, using your hands to fluff your energy.

Celtic weave: This is another one of Donna Eden's activities she has on video, where you trace large figure eights into the energy field, starting from the feet and working your way up. This works with all levels of the energy system.

Your Space

Create a home where you can relax and calm yourself while healing your spirit.

There are so many ways to cleanse your space. Each of these exercises affects the energy in its own unique way. See what you can feel before and after each of these activities.

Clean the unused space: Use the duster to move the old energy in your room. Dust your walls and the roof space, the corners of the room—wherever dead energy may settle. Try setting an intention while you do this.

Onions: Cut them in half and put them anywhere that doesn't feel quite right. Leave for three to four hours and then put in the bin. The onion absorbs any negative energy, so do not use these for cooking.

Fresh air and light: Open the windows and curtains daily and air out your home whenever possible. Bring as much sunlight as you can into your space every day.

Bowl of water: Try placing some large bowls of water around your house to absorb negative energy. See how it affects your energy.

Crystals: Place your chosen crystals with intentions in different places around your house, such as under the mattress or on the bookshelves. See more on page 120.

Incense sticks: Wave incense in each corner of your space, repeating a mantra or intent such as peace, love, joy, or optimism and clarity.

Fresh flowers: Place some fresh flowers in your house, whether from the garden or the florist.

Indoor plants: Look at adding terrariums, succulents, or any simple indoor plants in to your space to cleanse the air and energy.

Make it yours: Surround your space with things you love. Photos, art, knickknacks . . . whatever reminds you of the people and moments that you love.

Declutter

first decluttered my home and was surprised to find my space felt so much lighter and I felt centered. It truly is a magical sensation. I do this now whenever I get a chance.

First step is to head to your wardrobe. Take all the clothes out, popping them on your bed. Hold each piece in your hands and look at them with your heart.

Ask: "Do I feel happy when I see this?"

Start off with keeping the things you love. It is much easier to pick the clothing that doesn't feel right after you have held something you love.

If you have bought something, taken it home, and then realized it is not for you . . . give yourself permission to let it go. It has done its job by letting you know that you do not need it in your life any-more.

If someone gave you a gift that you do not like, it is time to let it go. The gift was in the act of giving the item to you, not making you suffer by keeping it in your home.

You are clearing away energy that is affecting you on a subtle level, and yet the end result can have a huge impact!

READY TO LEARN MORE?

Read *The Life-Changing Magic of Tidying Up* by Marie Kondo.

Energy Testing

uscle testing is an easy way to get a visual indication of your body's energy and what affects its strength. Try holding different foods, and, using a water jug, you can see how these foods can affect your physical energy, either making it stronger or weaker. This is a way to start playing with muscle testing while seeing what food your body actually wants.

Start with a glass or ceramic jug/bottle and fill it with water half-way.

The way to test if you have the right weight is to think a happy thought (beach, cocktails, sunshine, travel) and lift the jug. It should be relatively easy to lift—approximately 11–12 inches (30 cm) or more off the counter. If it isn't, pour out some of the water.

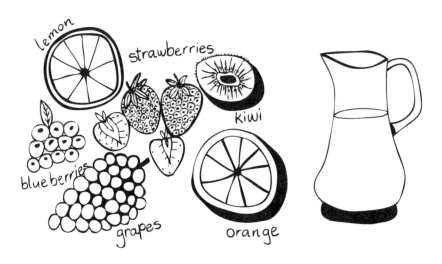

Now think a sad thought (death or war) and try to lift it. The jug should lift up only to about 2 inches (5 cm) from the bench, if you can lift it. If not, try adding some water so it is a bit heavier. Play with the water amount until you have found the right weight.

Now for the fun part. Pop into the kitchen and hold any type of food in one hand; relax and then try lifting the water jug. A high lift is a yes; if you can barely lift the jug, it is a no. Try statements such as "My body enjoys this. My body wants to eat this now. My body would like to eat this today."

Start at breakfast and see what your body feels like. Test your tea, coffee, muesli, milk—whatever is on the menu for the day.

READY TO LEARN MORE?

Read more about this in the book *Energy Medicine* by Donna Eden.

Ask questions without holding food, and lift the bottle for answers (e.g., think of a sandwich or your lunch idea).

Compare what your body wants vs. your soul (e.g., "My soul would like me to eat this now"). You may find your body is happy with any sugar at 3 p.m., while your soul may recommend something else. Also your soul is happier to relax and enjoy a drink or dessert when your body is not interested.

Next, try your toiletries, vitamins, water, laundry powder, or anything that interacts with your body to see if it is affecting your energy in a good way.

Essential Oils

h, how I love essential oils. I have found these to be such an incredible tool for cleansing my space, for healing my soul, and for calming or clearing out emotions I no longer need. Plus you can have so much fun with them!

If you don't have any oils, you can get basic ones from the supermarket, such as lavender or eucalyptus. You will find a larger variety from the health food shop or pharmacist or online. Just make sure they are essential oils and not fragrance oils.

Use your intuition to put together a blend of essential oils for today. Ask your intuition what will best assist your body to feel (fill in the blank—e.g., rested, clarity, or energized). You can also make a blend for your family or home. Whatever you feel you need at this time, feel your way through your oils to make the blend.

Hover your hand over your oils and see which bottles you feel drawn to. Put these next to your diffuser or burner.
Use body swaying to check how many drops of each you need.

You can look up on the internet your essential oils and their aspects for emotional healing. I also thoroughly enjoy the book *Essential Oils and Emotions* by Enlighten for information on the oils and what they are useful for.

Nourish Yourself

iving time to love your body can seem like a big task, and yet it can actually be really simple to do. I feel like the more love and time you can give to your body, the more you appreciate all that it does for you, from providing nutrients, allowing you to dance, laugh, cry . . . basically experience the world physically. Here are a couple of ways to connect with your body and give it more love. Before you begin, set an intention of what you would like to feel or achieve with this blend/massage.

Massage oil: This can be booking a massage, or as simple as using a massage oil and rubbing your calf muscles, shoulders, or feet after a shower or bath. You can even make your own with essential oils and almond or coconut oil. Just check what is a safe dilution ratio with the oils you have chosen.

Bath tea: Using epsom salts with herbal tea such as chamomile or green is a simple way to lie back and calm your nervous system while caring for your body. Muscle-test what you need to pop together in your own bath tea.

Body scrubs: Pop in your blender oats and raw sugar before mixing with olive or grapeseed oil and then add your choice of essential oils. It is so important you set an intent before making these. One of my faves was the Divine Moon blend, for when you are ready to scrub away your fears and pains and connect with what makes you feel whole, or the New Dawn scrub, when you are ready for a fresh beginning to start anew.

lavender

Signs

 here are moments in life when you can connect with what the universe has to offer, and a sign magically appears.

Ask for something to pop into your world today.

Perhaps a white feather, a special stone, a song that makes your heart sing, or a special number on the bedside clock.

It could be a song on the radio, a butterfly, or your favorite animal.

Have some fun with it . . . a little red car equals abundance in your life, or yummy food will somehow just land in your world.

Ask for a sign that makes you feel connected with your guides or able to hear your intuition. Even a reminder of those you miss and wish to hear from again.

It could be a phone call from a loved one, a surprise gift, a friendly visit, a bunch of beautiful roses, a gorgeous sunset, or something yummy to eat.

Ask for a sign that resonates within you, and then let the magic unfold on its own.

Love Strands

et's practice with psychic cords. These are like small hoses that psychically connect two people who then direct energy between each other.

The people you love are connected to you by these cords, filled with memories and joy. However, these cords can be affected due to negative conversations or just simply not seeing eye to eye.

Visualize this connection between yourself and someone who pops into your mind. Imagine blasting a cleansing water through this cord like a fire hose, completely removing any residual angst.
Next connect yourself (see page 28) and visualize pushing love from the very beginning of the cord all the way to the other person. While doing this, remember a joyful moment you have shared or what you love about them.

Continue this for as long as you wish. You should find that the next time they pop into your mind, your heart feels lighter. You can do this whenever you wish, with family members, friends, or anyone you really care about.

Ready to learn more?

Try an energetic conversation with this person. Visualize sitting down with this person and discussing heart to heart what is bothering you (see page 142 for more ideas).

Release Control

y family and I took a one-month holiday driving across Australia. It was an amazing adventure, and, after a month off, I was enjoying this relaxed way of life, taking one day at a time with no real schedules or to-do lists.

I asked the universe for a way I could live my life like this. And, yes, this is now how I live my life. I found the universe is incredibly efficient, and I can tick off two or three things I need to do at one time. Not just things that need to be done, but beautiful reminders also: an old photo, some gorgeous words, or something I'd forgotten or thought I'd lost.

1. Release any fears you have related to this idea, such as fear of being late, saying no, or forgetting something (see page 154 for ways to release beliefs).

2. Go through your to-do list, using the Intuitive Cards on page 104. Write down your list entries on separate pieces of paper and see how you feel about actually doing them. I found that what hadn't been done had a reason, such as everything wasn't in place to make it happen.

3. Hand over control. Use the universe to-do list activity on page 50 to ask for assistance on issues occurring at times when you don't know what the next step will be or you are just feeling overwhelmed. I did this with my entire list and watched the fun and playful ways my list started to get done without me even thinking or trying.

Rune Stones

his is a beautiful intuitive tool that has been around for centuries. Each stone has a carved Nordic symbol on it. This alphabet of symbols represents meanings and different energies. They are a perfect tool to play with your intuition as you reach into each stone for more meaning.

Casting stones: Place your hand into your bag of rune stones and pull out however many feels good. As you "cast" or release these in front of you, there will be a selection that is faceup. Your reading will be based on just these stones.

Use your pendulum: Some of the stones can be read as being reversed if they are upside down. Also there can be some significance if some stones land close together. Try using your pendulum above the stones to see if there is any significance or reversals for you to pay attention to.

Intuitive reading: Take the title of the rune stone and then write your own meaning for this reading. As you perform more readings, you will end up with your very own handbook of answers. If you need help from the guidebook that usually comes with the stones, begin there.

Past—present—future: A simple reading is to choose three stones as your past, present, and future of a current situation. Use these stones to give you more insight.

Book Games

 hen I am in need of guidance, I delve into my book collection and see what comes through. Feel for a nudge from your intuition through one of your books. There might be a particular book that comes to mind, or just an area in your house.

Follow whatever feels right, and see where you get pulled. Choose a book and, with it in your hands and your eyes closed, turn the pages until it feels right to stop.

You may feel a warmth or a joy-filled emotion as a sign. With your eyes still closed, move your fingers along the page until you find what feels happy or light, a nice buzz.

Open your eyes to see which words you have been guided to.

Always follow your heart as it knows the way and allow it to guide you forward in your life. Allow your life. Allow you compass to direct you on internal amazing path forward. Everything you need to know is inside of yourself.

READY TO LEARN MORE?

This is a great activity next time you are in your local library. You may ask for what your soul wishes to see or something to laugh about. Even a book your soul would love for you to read. Follow your intuition and see where it guides you.

Open to the contents page of this book. With your eyes closed, run your fingers down the list until you feel drawn to a particular page or sentence. Open your eyes to see what you have landed on.

Love Your Style

eady for your intuitive makeover? You can have fun with all the below activities relating to hairstyles, accessories, and makeup. There is something very comforting about developing your own style and feeling comfortable with your choice of appearance.

What do you love: Look in your wardrobe and jewelry collection to see what items you love. What is it that you love about it . . . Is it comfort? Its uniqueness or how it feels? Focus on what you enjoy about these items and ask the universe for more of these.

New outfits: Ask the universe for new fun ways to mix and match your existing wardrobe. See what you are drawn to each day intuitively, and celebrate each new creation.

What is your style?: Have a look around you for inspiration—either on the street, at the shopping center, or online at something like Pinterest. Put together a virtual or visual idea of your favorite kind of clothes and then ask the universe for these styles to be easy to find. Have fun—ask for them to be on sale or even at the op shop.

Sense of touch: Start feeling your way through different clothing. How will the fabric feel against your skin? Feel your fabrics, especially bamboo, recycled, or organic types, and see if there is one your skin prefers.

Declutter: Go through your bathroom, and ditch all the things that no longer bring you joy. All the old makeup, toiletries, or perfume that you haven't used in years—it is time to say goodbye!

Feeling Good

The more time you can spend in your body and out of your mind, the easier it is to hear your intuition. These are some simple activities to connect with your body.

Intuitive stretching: You can do this wherever you wish. Start wherever you feel tense, and move your body in whatever way that feels good. Your shoulders, your back, your legs . . . just start arching, rotating, and lengthening however feels good.

Yoga: Some styles of yoga are gentle and relaxing while others are fast-paced and energetic. You can try yoga at home as you wake up or before you go to bed. Search online for video tutorials that suit your style, or join a local class.

Tai-chi: The purpose of tai-chi is to develop the qi or life energy within us to flow smoothly and powerfully. There are a variety of videos online to see what suits you. Also have a look Qigong for shorter exercises.

Go for a walk: Find a beautiful park or walking area you can take yourself for a walk. Disconnect from your mind and enjoy your surrounds, whether it is the birds, the smells, the sky, or the trees. Whatever helps you unwind and feel relaxed.

Dance: Have a boogie in the lounge room. Pop a favorite song on, loosen up your body, and dance your heart out.

Creativity

hink back to when you were a child and creating was for the pure joy of it. You painted because it was fun. You drew because the pens were colorful. Remember a time when you loved playing and creating.

Today there is no need to limit yourself. Let's create purely for the sake of creating.

The first part is to clear any expectations; just allow your creativity to truly express itself regardless of your skill level.

Bring back the fun with creating, just like we did as kids.

Your creative project:
- Follow what feels good without any plans.
- Listen to your intuition and gut feeling.
- Enjoy as what you are creating unfolds in front of you.
- Step back and admire what you have created.
- Celebrate and congratulate yourself for trying something new.

Ideas for today:
- Make something with clay.
- Create a photo or picture wall.
- Take photographs of whatever you find beautiful.
- Write a poem or short story.
- Free-dance to a favorite song.
- Doodle on a notepad.

- Make your own jewelry with feathers.
- Try blackboard art.
- What can you make with "junk" from around you?
- Make different shadow puppets.
- Head out for the day, looking out for inspiration.
- Write a list of words that come to mind.
- Make up a song.
- Use paint to create your favorite color.
- Design what you would love on your own T-shirt.
- Create a dream board.

Manifesting

his simple exercise makes the world become a whole new magical place. It made me really believe we are capable of so much and can have what we really desire land in our world—somehow.

It was when I started setting a daily intention that I truly started to see how the magic could play out. And I also began to see how some desires landed relatively easily while many still eluded me. This led me to try to understand the technique and what worked well and what I was overlooking.

I found that the best way to start off was simple desires that I didn't mind whether they landed or not. Once I was comfortable manifesting my simple desires in my day-to-day life, then I moved on to the more life-changing manifesting and how to land my great desires.

So let's start off with a list of what lights you up:

1. Believe all the things are possible without you having to act to make them happen.
2. Think about what you wish to see land in your world. Start with something clear and specific, such as dangling leaf earrings or a dessert that you do not have to pay for.
3. Release any fears or hesitations. Know the universe will make this happen if it is meant to happen at the most perfect time. It is important you release any need for this to happen also.

That's it.

Now continue on about your life and just see what happens.

The first thing I ever tried to manifest was a pair of black thongs, my size for free—maybe a month later, a new pair in my size got left behind in our motel courtyard.

I remember I was away with my mum and my kids. We were thinking what we wanted to do for dinner. After a harrowing day of people and full carparks, I decided I wanted a super-close park, something where we could all have fun and we had options for dinner. We were on the Gold Coast, and it was busy. As we drove into the main town area, I got guided to the esplanade, and a carpark appeared three spots from the main dining precinct. As we parked and walked across the road, we saw an arcade filled with fun games and a food court with so many options for dinner.

Another weekend away with a girlfriend, we were on the hunt for beautiful clothes that made us feel sexy, and a cheap price tag. As we turned the corner, we found a boutique store with half-price clothes and a huge collection of styles we adored.

The secret is not hanging on to the end result with too much emotion. A great way to ask is "Wouldn't it be great if——" and then fill in the blank with your desire. Then go back to whatever you were doing before. I think of it like an experiment, and I just get to watch what happens.

Ideas for you to manifest:

- food shopping under a dollar amount
- a parking space exactly where you want to be
- a fun night out with your friends or family
- a gift from a friend
- to learn a new skill
- something you want to buy goes on sale
- a new yummy, healthful lunch option
- a sign from the universe that everything is okay
- a photo you love
- a phone call or visit from someone you love
- a new activity you and your friends/family will love
- a yummy recipe

READY TO LEARN MORE?

Write down a manifesting bucket list. Whatever your heart desires to land into your world. Think of the last time you said, "I would love to try that" or "I want one," or anything you feel an emotional connection to. Write these all down and just wait and watch. Check your list every month or so and see what has arrived off your list.

Set an intention each day when you wake. It may be time with someone you love, a heartfelt conversation, time with the kids seeing them happily playing, or a moment where you feel content or lucky. Whatever makes you smile about it arriving into your world.

Dreaming

our soul is freed each night to explore the spiritual realm. In your dreams, you have the ability to fly, to connect with people who have passed, or to visualize scenes that are impossible in your life.

Make a wish: Write down on a Post-it note or a piece of paper what you would like your dream to provide guidance on.

Connect with those passed: Dreams are a beautiful way to reconnect with those who have passed away. You will find them healthy, happy, and very much themselves. Think about how nice it would be to see someone you love again and then release this thought.

Dream journal: Pop a book beside your bed to write down any dreams you remember. You can even keep a space to write down the meaning as it came to you later with a second column or writing on every second page.

Prophetic dreams: This is where you get a glimpse into the future, often your own. Check your journal next time you have a déjà vu feeling.

Lucid dreaming: When you become aware you are dreaming and continue the dream in whatever way you choose, this is called lucid dreaming. You can fulfill your fantasies and consciously create whatever you can dream.

Intuitive Cards

tart by taking a handful of small pieces of paper to act as cards, and write down something you are undecided about or looking for more guidance on.

Whether it is a person in your life, an event, or a business idea . . .

Whatever pops into your mind. Write down at least half a dozen to start with. Even better, get a close friend to write down a selection of random ideas for you. This way you have no idea what could be written on them.

Shuffle them and pick one out without looking. Place your hand over the top and see what feelings come to mind.

Allow whatever images, words, or thoughts that enter your mind to freely come through.

You may even feel a physical sensation within your body.

Allow whatever thoughts you have to come through. Just free yourself of any expectations and feel free to express whatever thoughts or emotions come through.

Once you feel ready, flip the card over to see what it says.

READY TO LEARN MORE?

Try thinking of how you feel about these emotions:

Are you in this feeling or looking at it?

How do you feel when you take your hand off the card?

Do you want this in your life?

Do you feel a slight edge or something with the happiness?

Focus on the emotion and see if any further information comes through.

Is there something you can change to make this card feel better?

Ask how a different person may feel about this topic?

I love playing this with a friend. Try writing different cards for each other.

Mix a handful of your questions with a friend's, and both put your hands on the card. Compare what you get between you.

Experiment with writing down places, objects, emotions, and people in your lives.

And have fun! This is such a great game to really build your intuition.

Friendships

y favorite way to learn about any of these spiritual topics is with a friend or partner. My bestie, Cheriee, and I discovered we had similar psychic stories. We created many intuitive games and exercises to grow our abilities. As you explore these topics with a friend, you will find you both have your areas that you are intrigued with and can bring a different perspective to each situation.

What am I thinking? This is a fun, simple game you can play next time you are hanging out. Try to think of a place, scenario, or emotion while the other clears their mind and then describes whatever they see or feel. There is no right or wrong in this situation, so feel free to express any feelings or visions and then compare your thoughts on what this could mean.

Intuitive cards: This is a hoot between two people. Try visualizing any images or stories that come through. See page 104 for full details.

Past lives: Cheriee and I came up with this game together, and we found it was so handy to have someone else to ask questions. See page 151 for this activity.

Intuitive Business

he fun part about using your intuition in your line of work is playing in new uncharted spaces. This is where you can combine a number of your gifts and passions to create your very own business.

This, well, can sometimes be daunting, and yet it is also an amazing adventure. Here are some of the tools that helped me find and trust my calling.

Vision board: Write down all the desires you have to land in your world and place them in a space where you can see them easily. It might be building a home, supporting others, or to having your business thrive. Whatever lights you up, and you feel excited about it landing in your world.

Intuitive cards: This has been essential to my growth as a business entrepreneur. Some decisions we make are very logical, and yet we may be overlooking a piece of the puzzle; how we feel about each decision. Write down all your ideas and strategies on individual pieces of paper (like on page 104) and then pop your hand over them facedown to see what you feel. This is going to sidestep your mind and get to the heart of how you feel about these ideas. Once you are clear with how you feel, turn the piece of paper over. You may be surprised at the results. With any negatives, ask your soul if there is something you can do with this to make this more positive.

Visualization: Imagine your business with 6 million dollars profit in the bank. What is your ideal business to make this happen? How would you see yourself spending your days? What would you do to bring more joy and expansion into your world? Home in on this vision every chance you can.

How to help: I read a beautiful quote by Anne Lamott. "Lighthouses don't go running all over an island looking for boats to save; they just stand there shining." Your soul has made the decision to stand up and carve out a new life for you. This decision alone is inspirational to many others. Keep forging ahead, following your heart in the many curvy ways it will lead you. You are helping so many others by showing them they can follow their soul too.

Healing Temple

This activity is a beautiful visualization/meditation where you can create your soul-healing temple. This is a magical space you can come to whenever you wish to heal your soul and energetic system.

First choose a natural space you wish to build this temple, such as a mountain, island, beach, or forest. Whatever calls you.

Then create your healing area within this space. You can include whatever you wish. An incredible view, a shower, a spa or sauna. Maybe a natural waterfall. Be as detailed as you wish with this area. Look at the floor, the ceiling, the doorway. Create your own ambience that calls you.

Now create a space where you can lay your body to be healed. I prefer a space where I can almost levitate and visualize my entire body healing energetically at a cellular level.

This healing temple is yours to come to whenever your body desires it. This can be done as a meditation or even as you drift off to sleep.

Oracle Cards

 found once I started playing with energy, I would feel different emotions when going through my oracle cards. Sometimes emotions as simple as happy or sad; other times I would see an image or I would feel as though a card was not good for me at that stage.

Oracle cards are a fun tool to connect intuitively with your soul.

If you don't have any, we have a printable set online that you can download for free on the erthn website (https://erthn.com.au//free-oracle-cards/).

1. Take the top card from your deck facedown in your hand.
2. What emotion can you feel? Is there a happiness, joy, pain, etc.? Even a simple "Do you like this card?"
3. When you are ready, turn the card over. Do you find a connection with your emotion and the picture or meaning?
4. Continue going through the cards in the deck until you find a card that makes you feel happy or joyful.
5. Now turn the card over. Do you find any resonance between your happiness and the meaning of this card?
6. Try this process again, seeking one card as your focus for this moment.

You can also try a layout with a certain situation in mind, such as a card to represent the past, the present, and the future.

READY TO LEARN MORE?

Read your deck: Hold your deck facedown. As you move through the cards, try picking up any differences. Do you feel an emotion or see an image? Whatever comes to mind, describe it out loud. Try this on a handful of cards.

Weekly reading: Let's plan out your week with your cards. Pick out seven cards, one for each day of this week. If need be, take a photo to remember which cards you picked.

Ask a question: See what card resonates when you ask a particular question. What card will help me feel better?

Another layout:
1. current situation or issue
2. external influences
3. internal influences
4. to release
5. to accept

Animal Guides

There are times in your life where you may feel like you have a shadow. A bird that pops onto your blanket, a dog that seems to know you, or an animal you feel an attraction to.

Animals are a beautiful way to connect spiritually with the universe.

Signs: The universe loves symbolism and will send messages to you through animals. Keep an eye out for which animals appear in your world. Looking for more meaning: pop the animal name in with "spiritual meaning" online and see what comes up and resonates with you.

Pets: Many psychics believe your pets have come into your life to help you with a particular situation. They also have a great understanding of what is happening at an energetic level with you. See what you can pick up intuitively about your pets and why they are in your life.

Animal spirit guide: It is possible that one of your guides is an animal. Do any animals pop into your mind as you read this? Have a look online for this animal with the words "spiritual meaning" to see what this means for you.

Intuitive cards: Try the cards with your animal guides. Write down your pet's name, any animals you feel an affinity with, or any signs, and use your intuition to feel what messages come through (see page 104).

Musical Moments

Music can have an evocative effect on our emotions and energy. Playing a song can lift you up, make you feel like you are no longer alone, and feel loved.

Let's pop together a few playlists with the help of your intuition. Think of what type of music you are looking for, and then go through either your own personal music collection or an online digital music website to play songs.

Transition: The first one is a collection of songs that can lift you from a negative mood. Start by going through your music, and using your pendulum or flick testing, ask your guides to assist you in putting together this playlist. Feel your way around, see what folders/CDs feel good, and follow the energy. This soulful playlist helps you transition from your deep emotions.

Uplift: Create another collection of music for when you want more energy. To lift you out of your chair and make you want to boogie.

Memory Lane: Ask for some songs from your childhood . . . or songs that remind you of any beautiful memories.

Cleanse: Find a suitable song to cleanse your space.

Have a giggle and see what songs land in your world today.

What to Choose?

e always have the option to either stay where we feel safe or take a step into the unknown. The fear can stop us in our tracks and make us doubt the people around us, the beliefs we hold, even the safety in our shoreline. It is when we choose to step outside our comfort zone that the magic occurs. It is like choosing to open yourself up to a brand-new chapter in a brand-new book, even if we don't know what the ending will be.

It can be exhilarating and terrifying all at the same time. But what is most magnificent about this is realizing you have the option to choose a new story. At any stage. At any time. And it might appear uncomfortable because you are choosing a different action or re-action. But you are also choosing to honor a new aspect of your-self. So as you become ready . . . loosen your ropes, pay attention to your horizon you wish to see, and cast off your boat.

There will be time for tea and looking over maps as well as wind and ocean spray in your face as you guide your boat toward the shores that light you up and expand your awareness. Believe in yourself, and the opportunities you desire will arrive no matter which way you navigate yourself. It was said: "What you seek is seeking you."

Light a candle and ask for all you desire to be shown its way into your world and into your sights.

Crystals

started collecting these in my space at home, whether it was a little amulet or from the markets or girlfriends. I had a beautiful, clear dream one night that showed in the first part a collection of stones like you see in a museum, in a dusty glass container with no relevance, and then it fast-forwarded in time to show these stones as beautiful prized objects lining the wall of a futuristic spaceship with elaborate stories of where they were from, as they hummed with an incredible pure energy. I just loved the idea that each of these crystals has its own story, history, and vibration.

See if you find yourself being called to a particular type of crystal or even a particular color. I find myself seeing what crystals are calling me and then either googling what meaning they have or reading them with my intuition.

Make sure you cleanse your crystals as needed. This can remove any unneeded energy that may affect its (as well as your) vibration. I do stash them everywhere. My children are continually finding crystals hidden around the house; I even use them neatly packed away in the motel and restaurant.

To cleanse them, I just pop mine out under the full moon next to the clothes line and then bring them inside the next day, setting an intention.

USING YOUR CRYSTALS

Intentions: Choose a crystal to work with, maybe on the basis of the color or shape you are drawn to. While holding it, focus on your crystal with a specific intention, such as "I feel content and connect with those I am around." State your desire out loud and repeat it until you feel the energy in the crystal connect with this intent. You can always use your intuition to guide you. Then you can pop the crystal wherever you wish to remind yourself of this intention.

Crystal grids: I remember the first time I made a grid. I organized a beautiful collection of crystals, and as I finished I asked my inner guidance what it thought. The answer I got back was surprisingly clear: the grid was pretty but lacked meaning. I do find it interesting how my intuition can teach me new ideas and concepts. I pulled the grid apart, then, setting an intention, laid out the stones again. This time, I was surprised how different this grid felt and even how it came together. I was tuning it to what I was feeling, and allowed the crystals to guide me where they wished to be placed, depending on the intention. This simple addition added depth and meaning to what I created.

Meditation: This is a way to make your meditation time interesting, to say the least. Choose a crystal that feels like it is calling you, and place it on your heart or in your hand while closing your eyes. Visualize taking a journey with it and see what unfolds in front of you.

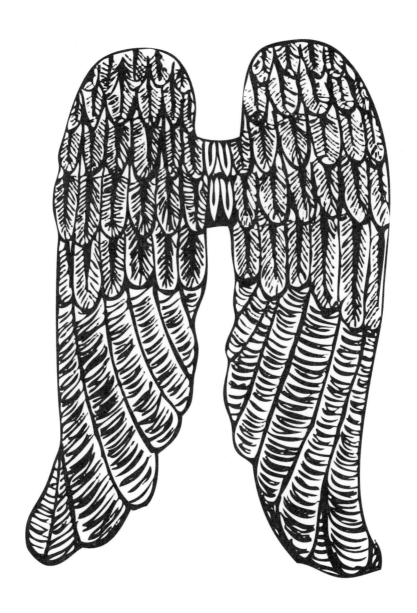

Angels

very now and again I will ask for assistance from an angel. One evening I felt overwhelmed lying in bed, and I visualized their big wings wrapped around me while I unashamedly hugged a teddy. I had actually borrowed a bear from one of my children's beds and hugged it so tight that night, asking to remember what it felt like to be loved and whole. The energy I felt returned was a sense of calm and love, that I had nothing to fear.

Another time I asked for help was with my baby son, who wanted his pacifier and cried into the late hours because it fell out of his mouth and out of his cot. I just remember feeling exhausted and needing help to be patient and loving while we all learned how to help him live without his comforting pacifier.

Angels believe in free will, so they will not intervene unless you ask for assistance. So make sure you ask! It does not matter if you are religious; angels are nondenominational and will assist anyone who asks. Whenever you pray or ask for guidance, you are tapping into angelic help.

They are able to assist with your everyday life, whether it is your health, family, career, or love life, or any situation you are wishing to change or move on from. Do not judge what is worthy of asking for help or not. Feel free to ask for help whenever you feel the need to.

Shadow Work

 hadows. They are those parts of ourselves we no longer want to allow into our world. It may be the pushy part of use, the greedy, manipulative . . . whatever word that makes you go "Nope, that is not me," this is generally a shadow.

You may also notice a trait of someone that drives you batty. This is generally a shadow self of yours too. If we work on the basis of duality, we have the capability to be kind and cruel, loving and fearful. It becomes a shadow when we say it is just not possible for us to be this characteristic.

The benefit of accepting that we are capable of a full range of emotions allows your to forgive actions of yourself and others. It makes everything less personal and just "is."

I love to think of our shadows as adorable, furry animals that we have shoved into an electrified jail and refuse to acknowledge them. Mine were wet and terrified of being hurt. This allowed me to see they really are harmless, and I was able to forgive them much more easily.

READY TO LEARN MORE?

Try a visualization that takes you to where your shadows are hidden, and ask them why they are not allowed out.

List all the words you refuse to acknowledge as you, and see the benefits (e.g., Bitchy = Knows what she wants).

Read *The Dark Side of the Light Chasers* by Debbie Ford.

Natural Connections

tep outside to clear you mind and reconnect with what is important to you. This is a simple way to clear your aura—and your energy.

Connecting: Get out to a national park or garden where you can get off the beaten track and sit undisturbed. Get into a relaxed meditative state. Sit on the ground with your hands on the grass or soil and see what you can feel, hear, or see.

Shoes off: Whenever you are outside, either in the backyard or the park, take your shoes off and feel the Earth. This is a simple way to ground your energy.

Full-moon cleanse: Stand under the full glow of the moon. Feel the light shine down onto you and into every cell of your body. Open the pores of your soul and feel the healing light soothe you.

Working with your plants: You can try muscle testing to see when they need water or if there is anything else they need. Remember to say thank you for being in your world, and share love with them as you can. Try to bring a few into your home however you can, whether it is succulents, terrariums, ferns, or plants in water jugs. This is a great way to bring harmony and revive your space in many ways.

Energetic Cords

These cords psychically connect two people who then direct negative and positive energy between them.

We are constantly creating cords with people and even animals and objects. These cords are not intentional, and whoever creates it may be completely unaware it even exists.

There are the gorgeous love cords filled with all that brings you delight in your relationship with another.

There are also negative cords which hold painful thoughts and memories. These can be created by a random negative thought, or by any issues you are working on, or from a history of conflict and negativity.

Sometimes I feel a sense of negativity that I just don't understand. You may even find a name or two pops into your head as you read this. If you feel negative thoughts when you think of a particular person, especially any that feel obsessive or fearful, this is a good indication that you need to disconnect from this person.

Visualize a cord leaving your body that you need to cut using scissors or a sword. You also need to imagine cutting the cord at the other person's end and either retrieving this cord back to you or dissolving it.

Shift Those Bad Moods

hen life feels overwhelming and you can't see the good anymore, it is a sign you need more self-love and trust. These negative feelings are normally because you are holding on to something that is not true. Here are some of my favorite ways to shift these feelings well and truly.

Cleanse your aura and chakras: Fluff your aura like a cloud (see pgae 71) and then ask your guides and soul to ensure all of your chakras are cleansed, balanced, and aligned with your soul.

Exercise: This is one of my girlfriend's favorite ways to cleanse herself. She heads to the gym and lets out all of her fear and aggression on the machines. It is also a chance to quiet her mind.

Have a shower or bath: This is my heaven. Create a ritual including candles, body scrubs, and chakra cleansing to reconnect to your soul.

Go for a walk: This is my go-to when I need clarity on a situation. Walking while looking at the flowers, the creek, and the sky, I find that in the calm, I get a better understanding of what I am looking for.

Ask for help: When you feel sad or overwhelmed, ask the universe for optimism and solutions.

Visualization: Surround your body with light, visualizing your heart opening more and more each time you breathe.

Meditation: I head to my bedroom, close the door, and zone out. I find this can really lift my mood (see page 60 for more).

Release: I write down everything that is eating away at me that no longer serves me: the negative emotions, the responsibilities I have taken that are not mine, the worries that I cannot control, and then I burn them (as safely as possible).

Boundaries

ntuitive souls can be incredible at understanding how others feel in any given situation. I found I would get so upset after an argument because I could not see how I could be forgiven. I could see the other person's perspective so clearly and yet could not see my own. It was at the stage I truly believed if everyone was happy around me, then I had nothing to worry about. What I realized was I was actually spending way too much time in other people's energy and not enough in my own.

Each time, I visualized myself returning to my own space. A simple check is muscle-testing your name. If you find you are getting a no to yours, it may mean you are currently feeding into someone else's energy. You can always muscle-test another name if need be, and then visualize returning to your own energy, cutting any cords as needed (see page 128).

I decided to learn how to strengthen my aura, so I created a boundary where I could help others and understand the situation, without taking on their energy or any issues that were not mine.

Filter visualization: Visualize placing energy packs around your body as a filter. I imagined these packs about the size of a brick around myself. They were filled with beautiful, clean, blue fluid that allowed through what I needed and blocked everything else.

Star Seeds

tar Seeds are those who hold a belief that they have lived on another planet or galaxy, perhaps one lifetime or even many. It was actually after I read an article on Star Seeds that I began to question if this was even relevant in my world. And as I began to look more into it, there was this resonance within my being. It was like what I was reading was so beautiful, and I connected with many of the Star Seed characteristics.

Star Seeds feel as though they have reincarnated on Earth with a mission to heal. Some other characteristics include feeling like an old soul, a sense of not belonging, and this sense of purpose of wanting to help the world but being unsure where to start or begin.

WANT TO LEARN MORE?

Look up names and pictures of Star Seed regions and see what resonates for you.

Write a story of what it would be like to live on another world, and see what comes through for you. I found as I did this activity, a story came through of a dying planet we had to leave behind and move our whole civilization. I was surprised how moving I found the story and the details that came through.

For more information on Star Seed families and soul characteristics, check out *Soul Mastery* by Susann Taylor Shier.

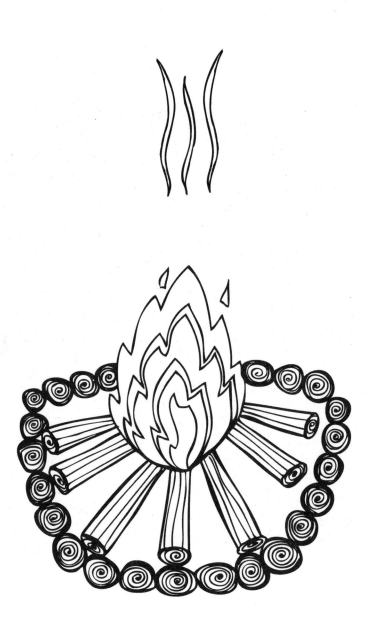

Write and Release

truly believe we can store in our body our pain or fear. Think of when you are having an argument and you throw out the main reason you are upset, and as the words leave your mouth, you realize that it does not sound anywhere near as bad as it felt. I believe once we can see what we are upset about, we can see it is not as bad as we thought. But when it is rattling around inside us, it can eat away at us. This is why you need to let it out!

Take a single sheet of paper and write down everything that is hurting, painful, or making you upset about the situation—every thought that enters your mind. Do not filter at all! It may come out as hurtling abuse or throwing out all the fears and pains that have been stored away.

Once you have written these down, take stock that you no longer need to carry these emotions. They are no longer needed in your world. Allow yourself to release this pain from your soul, heart, and mind.

With this sheet of paper, you can either:
1.   Rip it up into many tiny pieces and ceremoniously bin it.
2.   Throw it into a fireplace.
3.   Step outside and burn it in a fire-safe bowl.

Visualize this pain or hurt as no longer in your world, but instead as drifting away with the smoke or carried away with the trash.

Full-Body Scan

elcome to the temple of your soul. Not only does your body house your physical scars, but it also carries your emotional ones. This activity is to connect with your body and see what you can uncover.

Find a quiet space and follow the connection activity on page 28. Start at your feet and spend time with each part of your body, scanning to see what, if any, areas you notice. You may find a spot that keeps your attention just that little bit longer.

After you have scanned your body, place your hands on each part that came up, to see if any thoughts or memories come to mind. Ask your intuition if these are related to any of your emotions that need to be released. Delve into page 154 for more on clearing mindsets.

Use your visualization techniques to remove any fear or pain from this space, whether it is a cloud floating away or a piece of wire you can unravel or cut away from this space.

Use your body-swaying technique or pendulum to get more clarity on these areas and if you need to heal this area.

It is possible you may have to wait for the answers you seek. Ask your guides for clues or hints on where to head next if needed. The most important thing is to give your body love. Thank it for all the beautiful work it does (e.g., breathing, dancing, seeing), and appreciate how capable it is for you.

Clearing Visually

nce you get comfortable with visualizations, they can be a phenomenal way for clearing out pain and fear, understanding what is happening in your world, and also creating space for you to move forward simply.

One of the tools that helped me considerably was visualizing the issue or problem as a room with three walls, a roof, and a floor. And in it was all the stuff I no longer needed in moving boxes. Visualize getting a truck, stacking these boxes up, and transitioning them into a space to be taken away for healing. Empty the room completely without trying to see what is in the boxes.

It is important we don't spend too much time dwelling on the issues, since this can give rise to the emotions involved as well as the reasons you first thought you needed it. I really loved this visualization because it allowed me to move through these issues without getting caught up in the whys or hows.

Sometimes we need to understand a little bit of the situation, and as you are moving the boxes, you may even get a flavor of what the issue is about without having to look into it too much.

Another tool is placing your hands on each of your chakras and visualizing this as a room. What does it look like? You may find yourself in a castle, on a precipice, or in a rainforest. Get a visual and notice what is healthy and what is no longer serving in this space. Again, use your clearing-out technique to heal what is not serving, and repair whatever you need to in this space. Each chakra will have its own story, with strengths and areas that need assistance.

You can use these same techniques to gain insight into relationships through visualizing each person together. I imagine something like a chessboard, and place, for example, each person in my family onto the board to see what this looks like. I have found that each person will act or react in a certain way. For example, I visualized myself and my children on the board and realized that although my children were happy and content, I was in much pain; it was like I could not operate in this space due to old fears. I realized I was wanting my husband there with me or I was just not feeling confident. With this clarity, I could work through what was affecting me, and release the pent-up fears from my body.

Free yourself to play and explore in this space and learn more about what is happening in these spaces that needs healing or clearing.

Energetic Conversation

eady to clear the air with a friend or family member, and not sure where to start? This activity allows you to connect energetically and gain a better understanding of what is happening in your relationship.

I first heard of this activity from Jeffrey Allen, an energetic healer and trainer, and started using it to better understand my relationships. It was the insight of how they felt that blew me away. I really was surprised as to how much I was able to grow my relationships with the people I loved through this activity.

Find a quiet space and begin with a simple connection activity such as the one on page 28. Think about a person you wish to connect with, and visualize going into this conversation with the intention of clearing the air and understanding one another.

This is similar to when you have a conversation in your head either before or after an event; however, set the intention to speak to their higher self and visualize the other person's perspective as well as voicing yours.

Some simple questions may be these: "How do we improve our relationship?" or "What is the actual issue between us?"

You can also try this conversation with work colleagues, asking for a raise or even connecting with your collective audience or customers to improve your business.

Forgive and Let Go

here are moments in my life that I wish were different . . . the mistakes I made, words I wish I could take back, looking to others for answers when I wish I could feel my own.

When you remember your moments of pain or regret, you may feel a physical pain or a tension. I sometimes even felt flustered, unsafe, or unworthy.

And yet the reality is that these moments are no longer in our lives. We may even be completely different people from when these "mistakes" occurred. It is learning to see what served us in this space and release all else.

All of your past events make up who you are at this moment. It is the pain within the memory that is no longer necessary. Think of a person and situation related to your pain that you are ready to release. Visualize sitting down with this person and having an energetic conversation (see page 142 for how to do this). If this is related to you, visualize sitting down with yourself at the age you were at the time.

Feel free to let out all your hurt and pain in this conversation; however, at the same time, see what you can find out from the other person and what was happening from their perspective. The more you can understand the full situation, the easier it is to forgive yourself and them.

Try saying the *Ho'oponopono* prayer (the Hawaiian practice of reconciliation and forgiveness) to yourself and to them: I'm sorry. Please forgive me. I love you. Thank you.

With this new perspective, visualize the moment again. If there is still a painful emotion, it is now ready to be released (see page 58).

Every moment has landed in your world with a purpose, especially the negative ones. They are the ones that help us grow the most. Embrace whatever this pain or fear has taught you, and when you are ready . . . release it.

In Essence

A beautiful way to remember those you have lost is to set aside some time to just sit in the memory of their essence.

This is remembering someone who has passed, and visualizing sitting in their presence.

Find a quiet space where you will not be disturbed. Maybe flick through some old photos or even reminisce about some of the moments you shared together.

Take some deep breaths and release any tension you are holding in your body. Focus on their smile, the traits you loved about them, and what you wish you could say to them if they were here with you. Find something of theirs that you can hold on to to help connect with their spirit.

Remember what it felt like when you were with them, and invite them back into your space now, just to hang with you.

Think of where you hope they live now, whether it is on a tropical island, with their loved friends and family, or being younger and pain free.

Wherever this may be, send your love to them and remind yourself how thankful you are to have had them in your life.

Soul Pieces

 think of soul pieces as a part of us that runs away or escapes when things have gotten too overwhelming. It can be a part of us that is afraid of love or doesn't feel it is needed anymore.

There is a visualization you can do to retrieve your missing soul pieces, which is also known as a shamanic journey. When I take these, I am guided by my animal totem, either a whale or a dolphin. I basically jump onto their backs and allow myself to be taken to wherever we need to go.

For example, one trip was to a shipwreck at the bottom of the sea. My whale dropped me off and I wandered through, feeling which way I needed to go. This journey took me down several long halls until I reached a cabin with a young man holding a photo of his betrothed. He was extremely upset at the idea that he had let his young wife down, and seemed resolutely stuck in this space.

I have a conversation with each piece where I try to understand why it is there and what is important to it. And then I explain why I need the piece to come back with me, how it is necessary in my world, utterly missed, and a worthy part of my life. I visualize myself and this piece returning on my whale or dolphin to home, where I hug myself for its return. You could try your own visualization. If you are curious about this process and wish to learn more, Sandra Ingerman has a book called *Soul Retrieval.* I love what this book shared, and read it cover to cover in a weekend.

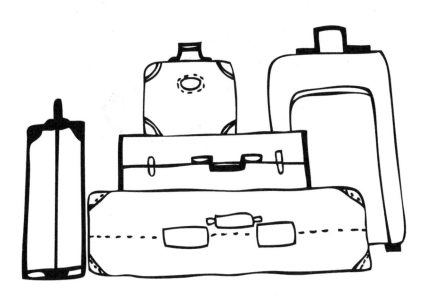

Past Lives

found taking a journey to a past life both mesmerizing and also incredibly insightful into where I am now. In saying this, I think it is important to realize that these memories are of another person having a completely different life experience. Take whatever gifts you have learned from this experience and then close the door on this life to ensure it does not affect your current life.

To begin this activity, write on a handful of small pieces of paper a collection of countries you connect with. Then on a second set, write down a selection of timelines (e.g., 0–200 years ago, 200–500 years, 500–1,000 years).

Now use your intuition to select a piece of paper from each collection. Place your hand on top of the paper and see what images come to you. You can visualize this as a story playing out in front of you. Ask the following questions:

* Is the message in the life you lead or in your passing?
* What comes to mind when you think of your death?
* Do you recognize anyone in this past life who is in your life now?
* See what images/stories come to mind. You may visualize a memory about this life.

When finished, visualize this person walking away into the ether and closing the door behind them, with only the strands of your gifts coming through.

Sexual Connection

his page is about finding your way back to the fun side of connection, discovering each other while trusting all the joy your body has to offer.

Explore: Your body is a road map to desire and passion. How well do you know it? Begin to understand what you enjoy, how you want lovemaking to be in your world, and what intrigues you. Embrace all that makes you feel sexy, and invite more into your world.

The Big O: Ask the universe for amazing orgasms or for your sex life to simply keep getting better and better. Invite fun by using your manifesting techniques. Put your desires out to the universe and watch what comes back.

Connecting: Distractions are a quick way to a fizzer in the bedroom. Focus on your partner and what you are doing at that exact moment. Think about what you are doing with them and how you would like them to feel. See how you can connect with them and with your thoughts.

Bring in desire: One of the biggest arousals for both partners can be interaction without any necessary action. Show your desire to your partner with your interactions. The way you slow down as you brush past or whisper in their ear. A cheeky message or a longer kiss. Make your desire known.

Clearing Mindsets

ll the activities in this book are assisting you in feeling your way to an answer. Really you are using your body as a way to access your intuition. We are going to use some of the tools you learned in the first chapter, to begin identifying beliefs that no longer serve you. Feel free to use either body swaying (this tool on page 39 is probably the easiest tool for this activity) or your favorite muscle-testing tool.

1. Choose an area where you will not be interrupted, and connect using the activity on page 28.
2. Use the Emotions chart on page 156 as a reference tool.
3. Ask if there is an emotion/mindset that needs to be released at this moment (either with body swaying, flick testing, or your pendulum).
4. If you get a yes, try to pinpoint the emotion by using the list on pages 156–157 (e.g., Is it on the left or the right page, then is it in the metal or the wood list).
5. Once you have an emotion, see if any memory is triggered by this.
6. Check if you need any more information to be able to release this emotion. If not, head straight to releasing the belief; otherwise, use your muscle testing to find out more, such as a date connected to this emotion, or find out what it it connected to, such as:
• Is this something from the last ten years?
• Is this related to a family member?

- Is this from a past life?
- Did this event happen at home? At school?

7. Generally, a random thought or memory comes to mind at this stage. If you come up with no idea what this is about, ask for more information. You may find you are ready to release with just the information you have.

Once you have all the information you need, it is time to release this belief from your body.

You have the power to release these beliefs with your words once you are ready, by setting an intent. "I release this emotion from my body." As you say these words, feel the emotion leaving your body. See the releasing page for more ideas on how to do this (page 58).

Now muscle-test again to see if this belief has been released from your body. If not, you may need more information to complete this. Ask your soul and guides for assistance on the next best step and release this over to the universe. Otherwise, congratulations! You are on the way to changing your beliefs and indeed your life. *Wahoooooooooo!!*

Emotions Chart

 hen starting to clear my old mindsets, I found having a list of emotions assisted in targeting what I was actually feeling.

The list below is sorted by meridians, which are based on Chinese acupuncture. They are energetic pathways in your body, which allow "qi"—also known as life force—to flow through your body. Emotions and memories can form blockages in these pathways.

Central: Shame, confidence, self-consciousness, overwhelmed feeling, vulnerability, embarrassment, shyness

Governing: Integrity, truth, harmony, humiliation, arrogance, enlightenment, success

WATER
Bladder: Pissed off, terror, horror, impatience, fear, frustration, dread, anxiety

Kidney: Anxiety, phobia, sexual insecurity, dread, fear, paranoia, disloyalty, carelessness

EARTH
Spleen: Confidence, empathy, cynicism, rejection, indifference, envy, brooding, low self-esteem

Stomach: Sympathy, worry, unreliability, fulfillment, nausea, doubt, disappointment, empathy

METAL
Large intestine: Guilt, spite, release, letting go, reason, sadness, depression, self-worth, vulnerability

Lung: Spite, guilt, release, self-worth, openness, humility, contempt, regret, depression, cheerfulness, grief

WOOD
Gall bladder: Resentment, bitteness, boredom, choice, helplessness, forbearance, self-righteousness

Liver: Rage, frustration, distress, hostility, jealousy, transformation, vengefulness, discontent

FIRE
Heart: Joy, pride, self-confidence, self-worth, self-doubt, acceptance, compassion, security

Circulation sex: Creativity, stubbornness, renouncing the past, depression, generosity, tranquillity, hysteria

Small intestine: Vulnerability, shock, sadness, sorrow, nervousness, internalization, assimilation

Triple warmer (energy management): Resilience, muddled feeling, service, invulnerability, instability, balance

Moon Cycle

s a woman, I have been fascinated about the timing of our menstrual cycle, also known as our moon cycle, and I have been learning how our cycle can affect our emotions as well as our creativity (Day 1 = the first day of menstruation).

Days 1-14: This is the time for expression. Our energy is upbeat and outgoing. Dedicated to new ideas as well as helping those around us. This is the time to start new projects.

Days 12-16: At midcycle we are more receptive to others, we are willing to hear new ideas, and we are also more sexually attractive at this period, due to ovulation, which also is the time where our mental and emotional creativity is at its peak.

Days 16-28: Take time to look back on what is created, and review any required changes or adjustments. This may appear to be an emotional or unproductive time both internally and externally and yet is necessary and therapeutic to our needs.

The couple of days before and even during your menstrual cycle can feel as though the life force is removed from you. You have no need to fear or be concerned about it, if your energies or emotions seem to wane for a few days each month. It is normal to need a few days to slow down and rest more. Trust yourself and your body with what it needs.

Love Your Chakras

eady to learn more from your chakras?

Use body swaying to see if there are particular memories or beliefs that you can release from this area.

You can use the activity from page 154 to see what beliefs or memories are causing a block in your chakras.

1. Place your hand on your base chakra. See what emotions you can feel. It may be a simple happy or sad, you may see a color, or you could even have a memory pop up.
2. Ask if there are any blockages that need to be cleared with body swaying (use this list on page 156 as a prompt).
3. As you begin cleansing, you may find that a person or memory comes to mind. This is your intuition giving you an idea what this blockage is in relation to.
4. See what patterns you can find with the blockages (e.g., What memories seem to be related or cause blockages in your throat chakra?).

READY TO LEARN MORE?

There are many different reports on the total number of chakras. I have been practicing with fifteen in total, and then I found an article that said there are 114! Whatever your magic number is, ask your soul and guides to cleanse, realign, and balance your chakras so that you can see what differences you feel.

You Are Ready

eciding to live an intuitive life is just the beginning of an incredible journey. As you have discovered, the universe really does have your back, and you can begin to push your own boundaries, discovering many of your hidden talents and gifts. Your options are truly boundless. The highlight is connecting with the love from all of the gorgeous souls around you. You now know you were never alone, and your unique quirks are not only loved but also admired.

Continue discovering more about who you are and releasing any of the stories that no longer serve you along the way. You can play, create, and enjoy this earthly experience. This world is yours to explore. Your desires are not only possible but are looking for you as you are looking for them.

I realized the journey is where the joy is. Celebrate each moment you learn something more about yourself or those you love. Each time you look around and see just how truly lucky you are wherever you may be. Connect with those you love and feel their love for you radiating back.

Invite in the wonder and the trust that you have everything you need in your life right now to make this all happen. You have always been ready to take this soul-led adventure of yours.

You are infinitely loved.

Thoughts

Doodles

Thoughts

Doodles

Thoughts

Doodles

The Illustrator

Natalie O'Brien

I've always enjoyed drawing. As a child I loved writing and illustrating my own stories. I've always drawn illustrations to give as gifts and loved seeing my artwork up in the homes of family and friends. I started my own illustration business called Notable Observations while teaching full time. I loved to draw out the stresses of the day and always felt calmer after I could release emotions out onto the page. Notable Observations sold framed digital illustrations, which had accompanying stories that went with them. I also specialized in painting abstract paintings that featured in people's living spaces, which were customized to match existing furniture, color schemes, and accessories.

I drew my way back to wholeness when recovering from post-natal depression. I shared my illustrations in mini-art exhibitions in Brisbane and sold them too. As my teaching career merged into motherhood, I later shifted my focus into crystal and energy healing work. I continued to draw to record my growth and evolution into new priorities and focuses. In 2016, I began sharing some of my black-and-white illustrations on Instagram, which related to the work I was doing at Crystal Catalyst as an energy and crystal healer.

Shan stumbled across my Instagram posts and contacted me to illustrate a diary for her. We cocreated the 2017 magical manifesting diary together and launched it into the world. When Shan shared that she wanted me to illustrate a new book for her, I was super excited to support her in this venture.

Since illustrating the book with Shan, I've begun working with symbols, sound, light language, and light transference in a unique cocreated energy realignment system called the Reality Rewrite Journey. This system embraces love, empathy, grace, service, and compassion. I help people embrace growth, change, and soul expansion, but what I'm truly passionate about is people living their authentic truth in the world.

www.natalie-obrien.com.au | insta: @natalieobrienstarlight
or Fb: fb.me/liveyourauthentictruthintheworld

Keep Delving

This is the list of our favorite books and websites. Keep reading and questioning and find your truth.

Shannon's favorite books:

Emotions and Essential Oils by Aromatools

Ignite Your Psychic Intuition by Teresa Brady

Conversations with the Other Side by Sylvia Browne

Light Is the New Black by Rebecca Campbell

Seven Habits of Highly Effective People by Stephen R. Covey

The Complete Book of Chakra Healing by Cyndi Dale

Energy Medicine by Donna Eden

The Dark Side of the Light Chasers by Debbie Ford

Ask and It Is Given by Esther And Jerry Hicks

Soul Retrieval by Sandra Ingerman

Transformation of the Species by Jani King

The Camino by Shirley Maclaine

Out on a Limb by Shirley Maclaine

The Soul Searchers Handbook by Emma Mildon

Anatomy of the Spirit by Caroline Myss

Journey of Souls by Michael Newton

Stand Up for Your Life by Cheryl Richardson

Soul Mastery by Susann Taylor Shier

The Power of Now by Eckhart Tolle

A New Earth by Eckhart Tolle

Adventures of the Soul by James Van Praagh

Some of Shannon's favorite web hangouts:

RebeccaCampbell.me   Mindvalley.com

BiddyTarot.com   Ted.com

Natalie's favorite books:

The Universe Has Your Back by Gabrielle Bernstein

Rise Sister Rise: A Guide to Unleashing the Wise and Wild Woman Within
 by Rebecca Campbell

Tune In: Let You Intuition Guide You to Fulfillment and Flow
 by Sonia Choquette

The Archangel Guide to Ascension: 55 Steps to the Light
 by Diana Cooper And Tim Whild

*Thank and Grow Rich: A 30-Day Experiment in Shameless Gratitude
and Unabashed Joy* by Pam Grout

Whatever Arises, Love That by Matt Kahn

Shealla Dreaming: A Journey to Unlock the Secrets of the Universe
 by Simone M. Matthews

*You Are Enough: How to Elevate Your Thoughts, Align Your Energy
and Get Out of the Comparison Trap* by Cassie Mendoza- Jones

*The Secret Language of Your Body: The Essential Guide to Health
and Wellness* by Inna Segal

The Sophia Code by Kaia Ra

Dragons, Your Celestial Guardians by Dianna Cooper

Heart Thoughts: A Treasury of Inner Wisdom by Louise Hay

Spiritually Fierce by Ricci Jane Adams

Navigating Dimensions by Lisa Transcendence Brown

Everything Is Here to Help You by Matt Kahn

Crystal Goddess 888 by Alana Fairchild

Crystal Masters 333 by Alana Fairchild

Massive Thanks

I feel incredibly humbled and blessed for all the support I received to allow this book to happen. First a huge thank-you to Natalie, who imagined and created all the beautiful illustrations in this book. Thank you for all your beautiful moral support when I got stuck and for cheerleading from the side as we continued.

To my dear husband, Shaun, I couldn't imagine taking this journey with anyone else by my side. You have believed in me, even when I had forgotten to, and allowed me to follow my heart, never knowing where it would lead. I love you xxx.

To Cheriee: You, my dear, are a legend! Thanks for the laughs while we delved, healed, and manifested our hearts' desires. I am so happy to have you on this ride with me!

To Sarah, Jules, Annie, Deena, and Teri: Thank you for reading my drafts, for allowing me to vent, for reminding me to trust myself, and for sharing your hearts with me.

To Carey, Peter, Chris, and the gang at Schiffer Publishing: Thank you for believing in me and giving this book a platform. I am forever thankful for this opportunity.

And finally, to my beloved two munchkins, you have reminded me how much you already know, and how much more fun life is when it is unplanned and I could not have it any other way. I love you both to the end of the universe and back.

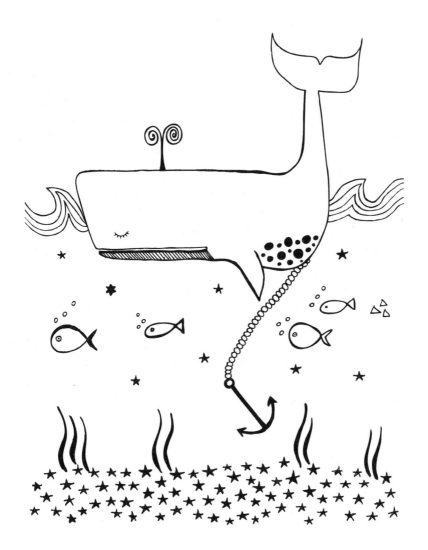

The Author
Shannon Cox

Shannon Cox is an Australian mother and business owner who was diagnosed with a stress disorder in 2013, leaving her unable to walk. With no medical solutions on how to fix this, she discovered alternative ways to help her recover the full use of her mind, body, and soul. What she thought would be a method of healing her body turned out to be a collection of activities to grow her intuition. This journey showed her that what she truly desired not only was possible but could also be manifested into her daily life and business. Shannon continues the adventure connecting with her intuitive self, and sharing new tools and ways to trust your soul at erthn.com.au.

www.facebook.com/erthn
www.instagram.com/erthnlife

She has also joined her dear friend Cheriee, to create, inspire, and learn more about their intuition while having much fun in the process. You will find courses, books, conversations, retreats, and much more at www.intuitivemamas.com.

www.facebook.com/intuitivemamas